The
FRIENDSHIP
BOOK

of Francis Gay

D.C. THOMSON & CO., LTD.
London Glasgow Manchester Dundee

A Thought
For Each Day
In 2003

The smile that you send out returns to you.

REACH FOR THE SKY

January

NEW YEAR is a time of looking forward, a time for sending greetings and good wishes to family and friends. Many verses have been composed to suit this occasion, but I think that these two lines, written years ago by an unknown Yorkshireman, sum up all we would like to say:

All gloom be with the old year past,
And this year happier than the last.

From the Lady of the House and myself — a happy, healthy and peaceful New Year to you all!

FRIENDSHIP is for young and old
Precious like a pot of gold;
Friendship is a sunny day,
*   As fresh and sweet as new-mown hay;*
Friendship comforts in the night
*   Like a star that's shining bright;*
Friendship is a gentle thing,
*   Soft as a dove that's on the wing;*
Friendship is a joy to see
*   And is the bond twix you and me;*
Friendship is there for all to find,
*   The secret saviour of mankind.*

Brian Hope Gent.

FRIDAY — JANUARY 3.

MY friend Eric is putting the words "do a good deed each day" at the top of his New Year resolutions list.

However, he intends to go about his plan quietly, remembering that fine Danish proverb which says: "Big words seldom accompany good deeds."

I wish him well in his resolve. Doing a good turn without shouting about it is one of the best resolutions to adopt at the start of any year.

SATURDAY — JANUARY 4.

BUSINESSMEN use the phrase every day. Men and women in government are rarely without it on their lips. In fact, it could be said to be one of the key phrases of our age. You may well have guessed what I'm referring to already, those three little words: "the way forward".

This expression is surely one that can be taken to heart by millions more than those who are in business or politics. It is an excellent motto for all of us in our daily life.

Onwards, not backwards, is the way to go.

SUNDAY — JANUARY 5.

FOR by him were all things created, that are in heaven, and that are in earth, visible and invisible, whether they be thrones or dominions, or principalities, or powers, all things were created by him, and for him.

Colossians 1:16

MONDAY — JANUARY 6.

"YOU never fail, if you never stop trying." Now, isn't that an inspiring thought to hold on to in the gloom of a January morning as yet again you face another Monday's workload or at home prepare for another day of challenges and responsibilities.

TUESDAY — JANUARY 7.

"WHAT a day it's been!" exclaimed the Lady of the House, as she sank wearily into her armchair. I agreed.

The weather had been dreadful — gale-force winds and torrential rain — the kind of day we usually choose to stay indoors. However, we had promised to visit a friend in hospital and to do some shopping for her first. The town centre had been at a standstill due to flooding which resulted in traffic jams.

When we finally reached the hospital building alterations were going on and patients had been moved to different wards. Even walking a short distance outside meant we were buffeted about and soaked to the skin. But Rosemary's smile and words of thanks eased our discomfort and we felt a little guilty about the way we had grumbled to each other on the way.

Home at last, warm and dry by the fireside, we could start to relax and I soon found myself humming that well-known old song: "Pick yourself up, dust yourself down and start all over again."

WEDNESDAY — JANUARY 8.

I RECEIVED a delightful letter from a reader who told me that she has her own tried and tested method of approaching each year's new Friendship Book.

Rather than, as might be expected, starting at January 1 she instead looks up all the dates important to her own family, acquaintances and friends and makes pencil jottings beside each. In this way, not only does she remind herself of all the birthdays and anniversaries for the coming year but, at the same time, she can gain special insight from the thought for that particular day.

Isn't that a lovely idea? Perhaps you might like to try it, too.

THURSDAY — JANUARY 9.

H ERE are some lines from that prolific author "Anonymous" which may help you get things into a clearer perspective today:

When you're lonely,
I wish you love.

When you're down,
I wish you joy.

When you're troubled,
I wish you peace.

When things are complicated,
I wish you simple beauty.

When things look empty,
I wish you hope.

FRIDAY — JANUARY 10.

A GOOD friend of ours, James, has built up a hugely successful business in recent years. He gets on well with his staff, his customers and his friends.

We were discussing things with him one evening and he said, "It's quite simple, really. At home, or at the office, I've found that a smile on your face first thing in the morning is really appreciated. Folk tend to be short-tempered at that time of day, and they are looking for reassurance that all's well with the world.

"Your smile has to be given when you start work. No good leaving it to the late afternoon."

What a bright thought! A smile not only makes the person giving it feel good — it makes everyone else feel that much better, too.

SATURDAY — JANUARY 11.

I CAME across a comment by F. W. Faber, a hymn writer, some time ago and although a few of you may already be familiar with it, it is so thought provoking I'd like to pass it on:

"Kind words are the music of the world. They have a power which seems to be beyond natural causes, as though they were some angel's song which had lost its way and come to earth."

SUNDAY — JANUARY 12.

JOHN answered and said, A man can receive nothing, except it be given him from heaven.

John 3:27

MONDAY — JANUARY 13.

SOMETIMES it seems that Winter will never end. Some weeks it can be cold, damp and dreary for days. Take heart — for Spring will come.

Be ready to spot the promising signs; watch for the first new growth pushing up through the grass, through the bare earth in garden borders, along roadside banks and hedges. Each day stems grow higher, and soon you'll spot the determined buds pushing upwards.

Perhaps the greatest miracle of all is the fact that from a small and delicate wild flower we have developed the magnificent blooms we can now enjoy in our parks, gardens and in bowls on window-sills.

Yes, the spectacle of renewal can be witnessed every year, giving us hope and reminding us what we can achieve if we accept the miracle and develop it further to a greater glory.

TUESDAY — JANUARY 14.

OPPORTUNITY knocks . . . and it could be at your door today. I like to recall the way people in China think of the word.

They say it knocks every day in life at your door and mine and, while some of us hear it, others don't. But it is not enough to hear the knock of opportunity. We must welcome him in, they say, greet him, make friends with him, and then all work together.

Now, isn't that a good way of approaching new opportunities?

WEDNESDAY — JANUARY 15.

SOME time ago David was told that the business he had worked for since leaving school was closing down. He said:

"It was a shock, Francis, for Alice and myself, and a bit frightening, too — we wondered what we were going to do. However, the village shop was looking for new owners because of retirement, and after much careful thought Alice and I bought it. It's hard work, and we still have lots to learn, but we enjoy meeting our customers, and they are so pleased the village shop has remained open.

"Alice said to me the other day, 'You know, David, the shop is really needed, and so are we.' It's a nice thought."

I nodded. David and Alice would surely see the wisdom in these words of the poet Tennyson:

Come my friends,
Tis not too late to seek a newer world.

THURSDAY — JANUARY 16.

TODAY is ours; what do we fear?
Today is ours; we have it here.
Let's treat it kindly, that it may
Wish, at least with us to stay,
Let's banish business, banish sorrow,
To the gods belongs tomorrow.

Abraham Cowley (1618-1667)

A Royalist and Cavalier, and a founder of the Royal Society, Abraham wrote poetry and prose, and was secretary to Queen Henrietta Maria, when she was in exile in France.

—

FRIDAY — JANUARY 17.

THE Lady of the House has a teacher friend, Yvonne, who, when working at an exclusive nursery school, one day asked young Caroline which member of her family would be collecting her at "going-home time".

"Oh! It's the repair-girl who's coming today," came the reply.

Out of the mouths of babes! For with her parents both too busy for that particular school-run, the au pair would certainly be the one to listen, sympathise and even mop up a tear or two.

Come to think of it, I suppose we could all be a "repair-girl" to any friend in need . . .

SATURDAY — JANUARY 18.

I WOULD like to share with you today this charming little thought. It suddenly caught my eye as I was thumbing through a batch of well-worn tomes in a second-hand book shop:

"There are many things in life that catch your eye, but few that catch your heart. Make sure you cherish those."

I found it a pity that the person who said that was not named. He — or she — certainly had a good grasp of what counts in all our lives.

SUNDAY — JANUARY 19.

HOLDING forth the word of life; that I may rejoice in the day of Christ, that I have not run in vain, neither laboured in vain.

Philippians 2:16

THE FRIENDSHIP BOOK

MONDAY — JANUARY 20.

ALTHOUGH I'm in a wheelchair,
I can hear and see,
So when you have something to say —
  Talk to me.

Don't ask the wheelchair pusher
If I'd like a cup of tea,
I'm in charge of such affairs —
  Talk to me.

Don't speak words above my head,
Bend down by my side,
I have so few things left to me —
  Leave me my pride.

I prefer to have eye contact
Than staring at your knee,
So if you have a smile to spare —
  Give it to me.

                        Ann Rutherford.

TUESDAY — JANUARY 21.

THE calendar, I'm sure we all agree, is a very useful tool, but here is a word of caution for us to keep in mind from the writer Charles Richard:

"Don't be fooled by the calendar," he said. "There are only as many days in a year as you can make use of. One man gets only a week's value out of a year but another gets a full year's value out of a week."

Isn't that something worth thinking about, next time you feel that the days are slipping by?

WINTER'S
MANTLE

WEDNESDAY — JANUARY 22.

SIR Isaac Newton, philosopher and mathe-
matician, wrote many inspiring things in his
lifetime. Here is one thought which I'd like to
share with you:

"I can take my telescope and look millions of
miles into space; but I can go away to my room,
and in prayer get nearer to God and Heaven than
I can when assisted by all the telescopes of earth."

THURSDAY — JANUARY 23.

A NEIGHBOUR who is proud of his Irish
family roots came round to visit one
afternoon and, as is his custom each time he
leaves, recited to us this Irish toast:

*May there always be work for your hands
      to do,*
May your purse always hold a coin or two;
*May the sun always shine on your window
      pane,*
May a rainbow be certain to follow each rain;
May the hand of a friend always be near you,
*Their hearts full of warmth and gladness
      to cheer you.*

Words for all of us to keep in mind.

FRIDAY — JANUARY 24.

DON'T be too busy, too serious, too sensible
to enjoy a little fun and laughter. Remember:
"A little nonsense now and then, is relished by the
wisest men."

SATURDAY — JANUARY 25.

IF, like many another person, you've ever felt homesick, take heart from this tale.

Jenny, a Scottish writer of our acquaintance, once found herself alone and homesick in the volcanic hillsides high above the tourist beaches of Tenerife. Persuaded against her will to visit an old Canarian mansion on January 25th, she was absolutely astounded to find the words of Robert Burns beautifully inscribed around the four cornices of what had, in years past, been the nursery dining-room of a Spanish nobleman's magnificent home:

Some hae meat and canna eat,
And some wad eat that want it,
But we hae meat and we can eat,
And sae the Lord be thankit.

The story went that the words of the Selkirk Grace had helped ease the burden of homesickness felt by the family's young Scottish nanny in the early 1800s. For Jenny, the poet's words, still shining brightly in that distant setting, gave her renewed hope and cheer.

May they also bring light into your life . . . that is my hope for you.

SUNDAY — JANUARY 26.

AND I will set my tabernacle among you: and my soul shall not abhor you. And I will walk among you, and will be your God, and ye shall be my people.

Leviticus 26:11-12

MONDAY — JANUARY 27.

ISN'T it sad when people, having reached a certain birthday milestone, decide that life holds nothing new, exciting or even worthwhile for them any more?

Far better, surely, to be like author Mary Ogilvie who, in the 1800s and having just celebrated her ninety-third birthday, saw her first book published! It went by the grand-sounding title of "A Scottish Childhood And What Happened After".

They do say that everyone has a book in them. Have you started yours yet? Mary Ogilvie did — and she finished it!

TUESDAY — JANUARY 28.

THE TRUE VALUE

"Of sentimental value"
Can often be a phrase
Describing the importance
Of a gift in bygone days.

Its cost may not be measured
In sizeable amounts,
But the personal connection
Is what really counts.

Thus "sentimental value"
Can often guarantee
Its true worth in recalling
A golden memory.
John M. Robertson.

WEDNESDAY — JANUARY 29.

THE great 17th-century writer Pierre Corneille wrote in his play "Le Menteur" — "The manner of giving is worth more than the gift."

Aren't these words thought provoking? They make a good thought for today.

THURSDAY — JANUARY 30.

WE all need to laugh, and it's even better when we do so with others. A joke passed on is a tonic and can do us all a lot of good.

Now, take this remark from a small child. Young Ross had proudly put on his new slippers. "Oh, Ross," exclaimed his mother, "you've put them on the wrong feet!" "But, Mummy," he protested, "these are the only feet I've got!"

FRIDAY — JANUARY 31.

I TURNED up some of the collected sayings of Confucius one day, and these words are worth remembering:

The best man is careful of these things:
His eyes — so that he may observe;
His ears — that he may learn;
His face — that it may always reflect kindness;
His manners — that they might show respect for other people;
His words — that they may be true;
His dealings with other people — that they may be fair.

There's a lot in that, isn't there?

February

A S you may know, the Lady of the House and I have Great-Aunt Louisa's fascinating scrapbooks and diaries in our safekeeping. While leafing through one of them one evening, we came across these lines by the Victorian poet and writer Christina Rossetti:

Love is like a rose, the joy of all the earth,
Love is like a lovely rose, the world's delight.

An unknown hand had added a little note underneath in attractive copperplate handwriting: "Grandpa and Grandma, who lived in London, knew Christina and her brother, the painter and poet Dante Gabriel Rossetti; their family was Italian. Christina refused two offers of marriage, and died unmarried. I remember enjoying her 'Goblin Market', when I was young."

Love is indeed "the joy of all the earth", and it is a pity that everyone in this world doesn't always get their share of it.

F OR we are his workmanship, created in Christ Jesus unto good works, which God hath before ordained that we should walk in them.

Ephesians 2:10

MONDAY — FEBRUARY 3.

I'D like to share this amusing and thought-provoking tale with you.

Following a lengthy meeting, three ministers were relaxing over a cup of tea in the session room when the subject of bats invading their respective churches arose. The first minister said that he and his beadle had caught the bats and transported them about 20 miles into the countryside, but when they returned to the church, the bats had returned before them!

The second minister said that he had done a similar thing but had driven 50 miles before deciding to release them, and they were back before them!

But the third minister said he'd had a similar problem but solved it in a more unusual way. He rounded up the bats, baptised and confirmed them, and they've never been seen since . . .

TUESDAY — FEBRUARY 4.

A SIGN OF SPRING

FIRST of crocus, fair and bright,
Cheering grey days into light.
Where the frost webs rib the grass,
Crocus greets us as we pass.
Sunshine beams the dullest day,
Hazy, in the season's way.
Is Spring waiting just ahead?
Yes! When Winter's hour has sped!

Elizabeth Gozney.

PEAKS OF
PERFECTION

WEDNESDAY — FEBRUARY 5.

DR EDWARD A. WILSON was a member of Captain Scott's National Antarctic Expedition in 1901. Not only was he a brave explorer and a fine doctor, but also something of a philosopher. One of his sayings is well worth keeping in mind: "Whatsoever things are of good report are worthy of your praise; whatsoever things are of bad report, are not even worthy of your notice, let alone your words."

Another of his maxims was: "Better to say nothing than to condemn, to laugh with, than attack and so, much happier."

A third comment is also worth sharing: "A happy life," he said, "is not built up of tours abroad and pleasant holidays, but of little clumps of violets noticed by the roadside, hidden away almost so that only those can see them that have God's peace and love in their hearts, in one continuous charm of little things."

THURSDAY — FEBRUARY 6.

JIM, a friend who recently celebrated his 80th birthday, told me the secret of his good health and lively interest in life.

"Put on a good pair of shoes and go for a walk," he suggested, "into the city centre or out into the countryside. If you are seeking new or creative ideas, just go out walking. You see, angels always whisper to a man when he goes for a walk."

The Lady of the House and I hope to be hearing our fair quota of those whispers from now on . . .

FRIDAY — FEBRUARY 7.

WAS there ever a more enthusiastic television presenter than Sir David Attenborough? His wildlife programmes from around the globe made him one of Britain's best-loved naturalists. Animals, birds, plants — whatever he was filming, large or small, he found fascinating.

At the age of seventy-four when asked if he was feeling like retiring, he replied, "Of course not. One cannot get bored by a bluebell!"

SATURDAY — FEBRUARY 8.

I'M sure that most of us have heard of Mark Twain, the legendary American writer and humorist — many of us have enjoyed his popular books such as "The Adventures Of Tom Sawyer" and "Huckleberry Finn". Twain, whose real name was Samuel Clemens, knew the value of enjoying the lighter side of life in his earlier work as a printer, gold-miner and pilot on the Mississippi. He wanted all his friends to see the humour in everyday events.

I was delighted to come across this quotation from the author: "Wrinkles should merely indicate where the smiles have been."

Some wise words for us all to keep in mind today.

SUNDAY — FEBRUARY 9.

WHEN thou saidst, Seek ye my face; my heart said unto thee, Thy face, Lord, will I seek.

Psalms 27:8

MONDAY — FEBRUARY 10.

"YOU like to learn new words, don't you?" I said to our friend Lorna.

"What have you found now, Francis?" she asked with a smile.

"Arctophiles," I answered and was pleased when she looked puzzled.

After thinking for a few minutes, she gave in and I explained, "It means bear lovers, the teddy kind."

We all laughed as we looked round her sitting-room. There were teddy-bear book-ends, a picture of a teddy-bear and, occupying a corner chair, bears of assorted colours and sizes!

"Well," she replied, "I suppose it does apply to me, but I prefer to be known as a lover of teddy-bears. It's much warmer sounding, somehow!"

TUESDAY — FEBRUARY 11.

FROM the corps newsletter of Plymouth Congress Hall comes this amusing tale:

Grandfather and granddaughter were sitting talking. "Did God make you, Grandpa?" the little girl asked.

"Yes, God made me," he said.

"And did God make me?" asked the girl.

"Yes, he did."

The little girl studied her grandfather for a while, comparing him with her reflection in a mirror.

"You know, Grandpa," she finally said, "God's been doing a better job lately."

THE FRIENDSHIP BOOK

WEDNESDAY — FEBRUARY 12.

TODAY are you meeting up with someone you haven't seen for years? Or is it perhaps one of those days when a person dear to you is leaving for a faraway place?

I always think that our feelings on such occasions are summed up so well in these lines which I found in an old album of clippings and photographs:

To meet and part is the way of life,
To part and meet is the hope of life.

Parting may be bitter-sweet but reunion calls for happy celebrations.

THURSDAY — FEBRUARY 13.

I THANK you God sincerely for the friends I
have today,
And all that they have done for me to help me on
the way.
I thank you that I met them in fellowship and
cheer,
And that in time of need and stress they always
have been near.

I thank you for my faithful friends in places near
and far,
Whose kindly deeds have made my days as
fruitful as they are.
Whose happy songs have done so much to make
my dreams come true,
And who, by their example, Lord, have drawn
me close to you.

Anon.

FRIDAY — FEBRUARY 14.

HAVE you heard of a lovespoon? It was a wooden spoon which young men in Wales used to carve for their sweetheart. It would be decorated with symbols: a horseshoe for luck, chain links to show the links between the couple, a heart for the love he held for her. A key meant that he wanted to lock the girl in his heart for ever.

Wasn't that a lovely custom?

SATURDAY — FEBRUARY 15.

I NEVER fail to be intrigued by the eye-catching posters which we sometimes see outside churches — you know, with amusing slogans designed to make us smile, or clever captions aimed at grabbing the attention of people passing by.

Perhaps some of the simplest and most encouraging words that I've ever read on a poster were those of George Craig Stewart who, as Bishop of Chicago, should surely have known what he was talking about:

"The church is not a club for saints; it is a hospital for sinners."

What a heartening way of putting it!

SUNDAY — FEBRUARY 16.

BEHOLD my hands and my feet, that it is I myself: handle me, and see; for a spirit hath not flesh and bones, as ye see me have.

Luke 24:39

MONDAY — FEBRUARY 17.

ONCE, when touring a monastery, I came on a painting of an outside doorway in a church I know well. A monk saw me looking at it and said, "I often pray before that picture. I love to imagine how the door will open to reveal the church inside."

Before I could check myself, I said, "But it doesn't!"

He merely smiled and said quietly, "For me it does."

TUESDAY — FEBRUARY 18.

WHEN Arthur and Maisie moved into their retirement bungalow, they were dismayed to discover that the back garden was overgrown with weeds. All the same, they were determined to do their best with it and by the end of their first season, were pleased with their efforts.

The previous occupants had put up a small greenhouse and builder's debris had been left in an untidy heap at the bottom of the garden. So, what were Arthur and Maisie to do? They decided the junk was too heavy for them to move themselves, so they did the next best thing — they used it as the base of a raised flowerbed and planted it with roses. Now they have been rewarded with a glorious show of scented blooms.

This story reminds us that we are not likely to escape problems but usually with a little perseverance we can overcome them or even turn them to our advantage.

WEDNESDAY — FEBRUARY 19.

A GREAT deal has been written over the centuries about folk who just can't make up their mind and who delay too long when asked to make a decision.

I think that some good advice on this theme is offered in a little-known proverb from Rumania: "The person who sits between two chairs may too easily fall right down."

THURSDAY — FEBRUARY 20.

SONG OF THE SEASONS

POETS write of Springtime beauty,
Others sing of moon and June,
Some will tell of Autumn glory
And how Winter comes too soon.

Every season brings us magic,
Wonder in the light and shade,
Nature gives us endless bounty,
Memories that cannot fade.

Sing a song of every season,
See the gladness all around,
Even in the darkest Winter
Still there's beauty to be found.

Moon and stars and clouds above us,
Sunlit day or frosty night,
Through the months the earth creating
Endless wonder and delight.

Iris Hesselden.

FRIDAY — FEBRUARY 21.

THIS anonymous "Thought For The Month" appeared over 70 years ago in a local newspaper, but is still as valid as when first written:

It is not easy
To apologise for a wrong,
To begin all over again,
To forgive and forget,
To control a bad temper,
To keep a high standard,
To remember that the sun will shine —
But it is worth while.

SATURDAY — FEBRUARY 22.

OVER many centuries great minds have often attempted to define the true meaning of friendship. For me, the words of Cicero sum it up beautifully:

"Friendship improves happiness, and abates misery, by the doubling of our joy, and the dividing of our grief."

It says it all, doesn't it?

SUNDAY — FEBRUARY 23.

AND the seventh angel sounded; and there were great voices in heaven, saying, The kingdoms of this world are become the kingdoms of our Lord, and of his Christ; and he shall reign for ever and ever.

Revelation 11:15

MONDAY — FEBRUARY 24.

DURING the Boer War a young English journalist was captured by the enemy and showed great courage in making his escape. The man in question was Winston Churchill.

Many years later, during the Second World War, he became Prime Minister, at a time when the outlook for Britain seemed extremely bleak. A great contribution made by him was the inspiration given to people by his memorable speeches and brave example. His words are still remembered and often quoted today.

One speech that is little known was given when he went back to his old school. The audience was expecting a great speech but he said only six words: "Never, never, never, never give up!" It summed up his entire message to his people in the dark days of war, and is still relevant to us today as we go about our daily lives.

TUESDAY — FEBRUARY 25.

I WONDER what kind of day you are hoping to have. My friend Robin used to say that we always get a choice:

"You can complain because the weather is rainy. Or you can be thankful that the grass is getting watered for free."

"You can grumble about your health. Or you can rejoice that you are alive."

The way each new day will work out depends rather a lot on us.

WEDNESDAY — FEBRUARY 26.

THE Lady of the House found this "Recipe For Happiness" in an old cookery book:

Take a cup of patience
And a big heartful of love,
Add a bowl of generosity
To blend with the above;
Put in a dash of laughter
And some understanding, too,
Sprinkle it with kindness
And memories old and new.
Add some faith before you mix it
Till the dish is rich and sweet,
Then enjoy a heaped-up portion
With everyone you meet!

THURSDAY — FEBRUARY 27.

HERE is a good piece of advice that has been passed on to me:

When you are under stress, remember the Custard Principle — don't get upset over trifles.

FRIDAY — FEBRUARY 28.

THERE was a popular song when I was young which said it all about happiness. It went like this:

I want to be happy
But I can't be happy
Till I make you happy, too.

Simple words, but a great truth. Make someone else happy and you'll be happy yourself! It never fails.

March

ONE of the popular TV programmes for many years was the quiz "Mastermind" with its question master, Magnus Magnusson. When time ran out for each contestant a buzzer sounded, but if Magnus hadn't completed the question he said, "I've started so I'll finish." It gave the contestant an opportunity to answer one more question and to increase their score.

The saying became quite a catchphrase, but it is a good motto for life, too. There is something rather sad about letting something we once started with enthusiasm remain unfinished. On the other hand, there is something immensely satisfying about a job that has been completed.

At the end of a life filled with many hardships and dangers, shipwreck and imprisonment, St Paul wrote: "I have fought a good fight, I have finished my course, I have kept the faith."

There's something to encourage us!

BUT Jesus called them unto him, and said, Suffer little children to come unto me, and forbid them not: for of such is the kingdom of God.

Luke 18:16

MONDAY — MARCH 3.

DO people ask you to give them advice from time to time? A friend who is often confronted in this way passed on to me these words of advice on the very subject of advice:

"It is easy when we are in prosperity to give advice to the afflicted." Aeschylus.

"Advice is like snow: the softer it falls the longer it dwells upon, and the deeper it sinks into, the mind." Samuel Taylor Coleridge.

TUESDAY — MARCH 4.

SPRING CAROL

THE sun streams through the window pane
My heart begins to sing,
A certain stirring in the air
And suddenly it's Spring.
Bluebells, tulips, daffodils
All show their dainty heads,
Whilst crocus cups and hyacinths
Adorn the garden beds.

The frothy pink of almond spray,
Primroses in the lane,
Proclaim the season of new life
Is with us once again.
Whilst overhead on blossomed bough
I hear a blackbird sing,
Pouring out in golden notes
Its carol to the Spring.

Kathleen Gillum.

WEDNESDAY — MARCH 5.

THE novelist John Buchan is remembered by thousands for "The Thirty-Nine Steps", a book that was turned into a popular film directed by Alfred Hitchcock. Buchan is also remembered for these wise words he wrote in "Memory Hold The Door":

"To live for a time close to great minds is the best kind of education."

This distinguished writer and statesman had more opportunities than most of us to meet and mingle with men and women of considerable knowledge and intellect.

THURSDAY — MARCH 6.

"COME and see this," said Mhairi's husband. Hamish had been clearing away a tangle of brambles and long grass from around the garden shed. He took his wife's arm and led her round to the back of the shed.

There was the small plot where they had so tearfully buried their beloved springer spaniel, Trixie, several years before. Over the grave was growing a beautiful wild rose bush, no doubt seeded by the birds which Trixie had loved to chase.

Mhairi gazed at the profusion of beautiful white blossoms and breathed in the scent — what a wonderful tribute nature had provided for a much-loved companion.

"I suppose that's what is known as a Dog Rose," she mused.

FRIDAY — MARCH 7.

A WISE friend of ours who lived to be almost 100 was asked on her 90th birthday what sort of advice she would choose to pass on to a restless teenager. Flora read out these lines by the writer Elinor Rose:

Enjoy your age before it's past;
Don't try to be eighteen so fast.
You're only fourteen once, my dears,
But you'll be thirty-five for years.

SATURDAY — MARCH 8.

THE courageous Helen Keller who, minus sight, speech and hearing, faced all the darkest moments in her own life, has left us with words to say over and over again to friends and family — indeed to ourselves — when gloomy days come unexpectedly upon us.

"The marvellous richness of human experience," she wrote, "would lose something of rewarding joy if there were no limitations to overcome. The hilltop hour would not be half as wonderful if there were no dark valleys to traverse."

May today be happy for you on the hilltop as you say thanks for leaving gloom behind in the valley.

SUNDAY — MARCH 9.

GRACE be unto you, and peace, from God our Father, and from the Lord Jesus Christ.

Corinthians I 1:3

MONDAY — MARCH 10.

I'M sure you'll agree that we're all guilty, from time to time, of concentrating on the negative side of friends and neighbours. You'll know exactly what I mean.

Here's a useful thought to keep in mind which has worked for me, and I am happy to pass it on to you today:

"Next time you start looking around for faults, be sure to use a mirror, not a telescope."

TUESDAY — MARCH 11.

THOUGH trying times can prove to be
A feature of life's constancy,
On looking round, one can't deny
The operative word is — try.

Try to lend a helping hand,
And always try to understand
No matter what may aggravate,
Try to put the record straight.

Try to formulate a theme,
That proves the basis of a scheme,
Whereby an optimistic kind
Of hope leaves lethargy behind.

Whatever path you may pursue,
Try your best in all you do,
And make it clear as time goes by,
The effort's always worth a try.
                    J. M. Robertson.

WEDNESDAY — MARCH 12.

HAVE you ever heard of the expression, "pie-crust promise"? I am quite sure that even if you haven't, you can guess exactly what is meant.

It refers, of course, to the sort of assurance which is glibly given and just as heedlessly broken. A promise which is, alas, as likely to crumble apart as the pastry of a pie.

And a pie-crust promise is the very opposite of my favourite promise. It's one which is given every year; never put into words, certainly never written down — but always fulfilled. It's pledged in the first bulbs peeping through the snow, in the budding daffodils standing bravely in the rain, in the catkins which cling to the tree, however turbulently tossed by the wind.

Have you guessed? Yes, I'm sure you have by now. It's the promise of Spring — that annual miracle which never, ever lets us down.

THURSDAY — MARCH 13.

WHEN he was 85 Pablo Casals, the great cellist, was asked why he still practised for five hours every day. His reply was, "Because I think I am getting better."

I was reminded of General Douglas McArthur who said, "Whatever your years, there is in every heart the love of wonder, the undaunted challenge of events, the unfailing childlike appetite for what comes next. You are as young as your hope and as old as your despair."

Inspiring words indeed!

FRIDAY — MARCH 14.

THE small son of a friend of ours will not go to bed until he has had his "choccy drink". It is to Christopher Columbus that the original credit should go for making known the secret of this popular flavour. He brought back cocoa beans to Spain after his fourth voyage to the New World in 1502.

Many years later it became a favourite beverage of the Spanish princess Maria Theresa, and after she married the Sun King Louis XIV of France, its popularity spread rapidly, helped by the tribute paid by an unknown Italian writer. In the course of an article on "occupational diseases", he declared that a chocolate drink "soothes the digestion, calms the intellect, and induces a sound sleep."

Many of us would go along with that.

SATURDAY — MARCH 15.

WORDS such as neighbourliness, enthusiasm, caution, conscientiousness, fortitude and urbanity — carry some weight in ascertaining human values, but without "U" and "I", they become quite ineffective.

SUNDAY — MARCH 16.

AND whatsoever ye do in word or deed, do all in the name of the Lord Jesus, giving thanks to God and the Father by him.

Colossians 3:17

THE FRIENDSHIP BOOK

<u>MONDAY — MARCH 17.</u>

T HERE are moments in everyone's life when you feel like losing your temper. I like, at such times, to think of my trusty dictionary and to look up the word "anger".

My friend Adam once suggested that we should simply prefix the word with the letter "d" and realise that such a fiery mood can, just as easily, spell out the warning, danger.

<u>TUESDAY — MARCH 18.</u>

I HAVE collected hundreds of definitions over the years of the various traits that go towards making people good friends. One day, I came across this, so different from many others, and yet so true:

A friend should be radical;
He should love you when you're unlovable,
Hug you when you're unhuggable,
And bear you when you're unbearable.

A friend should be fanatical;
He should cheer when the whole world boos,
Dance when you get good news,
And cry when you cry, too.

But most of all, a friend should be mathematical,
He should multiply the joy, divide the sorrow,
Subtract the past, and add to tomorrow,
Calculate the need deep in your heart,
And always be bigger than the sum of all
  their parts.

Anon.

TWO'S
COMPANY

WEDNESDAY — MARCH 19.

HERE is not one thought for today, but two! "There is nothing lost by civility" the saying reminds us, while Shakespeare wrote in "Othello":

"How poor are they that have not patience."

Patience and politeness — some call it courtesy, civility, good manners; they certainly help the wheels of daily life to turn more smoothly and more pleasantly. The world would be the poorer without these attributes, don't you think?

THURSDAY — MARCH 20.

AFTER weeks of cold, wet weather we had a sudden taste of Spring one day. The warm rays of sunshine tempted the Lady of the House and me out and we decided to take a bus journey. Soon we were passing green fields beside country roads. Rabbits were to be seen, as were lambs, bushes bursting with life, everything fresh and new.

It would have been easy to stay indoors, as there was still a chilly wind, but we were glad we had made the effort that day. Sometimes at the end of Winter we become a little lethargic, yet nature's treasure chest can always offer us a tonic.

If it's difficult for you to get away for a day or even an afternoon, why not spare a few minutes to look more closely at your neighbours' gardens? Watch for birds nesting or just have a peep in your local florist's window.

I promise you Nature's Tonic. It never fails!

FRIDAY — MARCH 21.

FEELING gloomy? Read this, and you may feel more light-hearted. One day I came across these thoughts on facial expression:

A smile is a silent laugh; a grin is a smile to yourself that shows; a chuckle is a small laugh, sometimes genuine, sometimes forced; a chortle is a wonderful word coined by Lewis Carroll of "Alice In Wonderland" fame, meaning a gleeful chuckle and a little laugh.

And a laugh, a true laugh — that is happiness set to joyous music.

May that joyous music ring in your heart today.

SATURDAY — MARCH 22.

IT'S good to know that you cannot always judge a book by its cover, and nor can you judge a man-of-the-cloth by his serious sermons! This was brought home to me when a local minister told this story against himself.

Noticing a workman climbing up to the roof of his church one day, he enquired about the problem in a penetrating voice. Quick as a flash came the answer from the man on the ladder:

"Well, you see, it's like this . . . I've been told there's a drip in the pulpit."

SUNDAY — MARCH 23.

SEEK ye the Lord while he may be found, call ye upon him while he is near.

Isaiah 55:6

THE FRIENDSHIP BOOK

<u>MONDAY — MARCH 24.</u>

ONE day when our friend Joan was visiting an elderly aunt, she noticed on the door of her fridge, not the usual collection of recipes and reminders held fast by fridge magnets, but something quite different. Her aunt had gathered snippets of inspirational verse and one in particular struck a chord:

How many go forth in the morning
　Who never come home at night?
And hearts are broken
　For harsh words spoken
That sorrow can never put right.
　We have careful words for the stranger
And smiles for the sometime guest
　But for our own, the bitter tone . . .
Though we love our own the best!

<u>TUESDAY — MARCH 25.</u>

I ENJOYED a chat over the garden wall with our neighbour John. March, which had come in like a lion, was going out like a lamb.

"A great day for gardening today, Francis! We must make the most of this good weather."

I nodded in agreement. Then John said with a twinkle in his eye, "Do you remember C. D. Warner's words on the subject, Francis? 'What a man needs in gardening is a cast-iron back, with a hinge in it!'"

I smiled. A gardener would, I knew, after some hard work appreciate the truth of these words, written in 1870 in "My Summer In The Garden".

WEDNESDAY — MARCH 26.

SCHOOLBOY howlers have long provided reams of innocent amusement, but what about the story from the other side of the chalk face, when a teacher wrote this end-of-term report:

"The recent improvement in Fiona's handwriting now reveals the atrocious nature of her spelling."

Isn't life itself sometimes rather like that? Just when we think that we've solved one dilemma, suddenly yet another problem rears its head. But like Fiona we must all persevere in the knowledge that there are inevitably further challenges ahead.

THURSDAY — MARCH 27.

"DO not seek God in outer space — your heart is the only place in which you meet him face to face."

Angelius Silesius.

FRIDAY — MARCH 28.

JAMES McINTOSH PATRICK, the celebrated Scottish landscape artist, loved welcoming people into his Dundee home. If the delivery boy brought his evening paper to the door when he had guests he was invited in, too!

He was treated with the same friendly courtesy as everyone else, encouraged to join in the conversation and comment on Patrick's latest painting. No wonder McIntosh Patrick was one of Dundee's best-loved citizens.

SYMPHONY
IN SPRING

SATURDAY — MARCH 29.

TODAY, like many other people, you may be feeling slightly discontented with your life. Are you preoccupied with the way people and circumstances seem to be treating you? Well, here's a thought to keep in mind, words from the celebrated American writer and philosopher Mark Twain:

"Don't go around saying that the world owes you a living. The world owes you nothing — it was here first."

SUNDAY — MARCH 30.

BLESSED are ye that hunger now: for ye shall be filled. Blessed are ye that weep now: for ye shall laugh.

Luke 6:21

MONDAY — MARCH 31.

TOMORROW will be April The First, the day when people with a sense of fun dream up and play practical jokes on friends and neighbours.

Those of us who have a good sense of humour tend to find daily life is that bit more enjoyable. The 19th-century philosopher Henry Ward Beecher said: "A person without a sense of humour is like a wagon without springs, jolted by every pebble in the road."

Others have claimed that a keen and ever-present sense of humour is a recipe for good health and a constant enjoyment of life. Laughter is indeed the best medicine.

April

TUESDAY — APRIL 1.

IF you've ever wondered as to the essential difference between perseverance and obstinacy, look no further:

"Perseverance is a strong will; obstinacy is an equally strong 'won't'!"

WEDNESDAY — APRIL 2.

THE Lady of the House and I once enjoyed a lovely Spring holiday in the Lake District where we walked in the footsteps of William Wordsworth and his sister Dorothy.

We visited the poet's birthplace in Cockermouth, then spent time at Dove Cottage and Rydal Mount. We also visited Ullswater, beside which William saw a carpet of dancing daffodils, later the inspiration of his famous poem "The Daffodils".

But it is another of William's poems, the beautiful "Lines Composed A Few Miles Above Tintern Abbey" which provides us with a thought for today: "That best portion of a good man's life, his little nameless, unremembered acts of kindness and love."

Surely timeless words to keep in mind as we go about our daily lives.

THURSDAY — APRIL 3.

I OFTEN wonder if we realise just how good health matters more than good wealth. The concept of total "wellness" recognises that our every thought, word and deed affects our greater health and wellbeing.

A friend once said, "Just as our cars run more smoothly, and require less energy to go faster and farther when the wheels are in perfect alignment, so we perform better when our thoughts, feelings, emotions, goals and values are in balance."

Isn't it wise to keep reminding ourselves that health is our real wealth, so let's keep ourselves fit for happy living!

FRIDAY — APRIL 4.

A SIMPLE PRAYER

I DO not pray for fame or wealth,
But this, Dear Lord, I ask:
Sufficient courage for the day
And strength for every task.

I may not have unfailing health
But this I pray You'll give:
A cheerful spirit, loving heart,
As long as I may live.

I do not pray for plans and schemes
Or dreams that won't come true,
But give me, Lord, undying faith
And keep me close to You.

Iris Hesselden.

SATURDAY — APRIL 5.

IF you ever become bored with life, think of the advice handed out by an old friend who was always full of the joys, as they say. Frank's tip was to be more active and go out to brighten up your community of friends, family and associates.

He later said that he put immense store by these words from the playwright and philosopher George Bernard Shaw:

"Rejoice in life for its own sake, for your life is no brief candle. Rather, it is a splendid torch, which you have got a hold of for the moment. Make it burn as brightly as possible before you hand it on to future generations."

SUNDAY — APRIL 6.

FOR many are called, but few are chosen.

Matthew 22:14

MONDAY — APRIL 7.

AN Irish friend, Patrick, always has a happy and forgiving outlook on the world and its ways. Once, when feeling particularly agreeable to all and sundry, he quoted this old Irish toast:

"May you never make an enemy, when you could make a friend."

Then he smiled and added the final line: "Unless you meet a fox among your chickens."

Isn't it good to share a sense of down-to-earth humour and enjoy these "words of wisdom" from around the world?

TUESDAY — APRIL 8.

DURING the early days of the Second World War, many public-spirited citizens felt the need to boost public morale by arranging musical concerts. The mayor of a small Lancashire town combined forces with the civic leaders of neighbouring communities to invite the Halle Orchestra, temporarily homeless after the destruction of the Free Trade Hall in Manchester.

At the end of January 1941, the orchestra gave a concert in the local public hall. Well over one thousand folk attended, the conductor's baton adeptly wielded by the redoubtable Malcolm Sargent.

It fell to the mayor who had initiated the concert to wind up the evening's proceedings. He was delighted, he said, to move a vote of thanks to Sergeant Malcolm and his band for this wonderful evening's entertainment!

WEDNESDAY — APRIL 9.

OUR friends George and Emily recently entered a very hectic time in their lives. They've retired and are busy going to classes, keen to learn all sorts of new things. Emily is doing a pottery course and George has taken up local history. They also go to ballroom dancing lessons together.

"We're not trying to recapture our teenage years, but we've now entered our *keenage* years," he says enthusiastically. "We've never been so busy since the day we gave up work!"

THURSDAY — APRIL 10.

I'VE been reading about Henry Thoreau, one of America's most respected and best loved writers. He was indeed a man of many parts — a scholar and teacher, a naturalist and inventor, a poet, a humorist and social critic. As a stalwart believer in human rights, he also found time to speak passionately against the slave trade.

Yet despite his enormous range of abilities and accomplishments, Thoreau came from humble origins, and continued throughout his life to deplore mankind's obsession with material wealth. One thing he definitely did value was the importance of human aspirations.

"If you have built castles in the air," he once said, "then your work need not be lost; that is where they should be. Now put the foundations under them."

Inspiring words from a most inspiring man.

FRIDAY — APRIL 11.

AS warmer, longer Spring days arrive, here's a delightful poem by Katherine White which encapsulates the new season:

It's snowing blossom down the avenues,
Magnolias unfold,
Forsythia challenges the sunlight
And trees burgeon.

Colours glint in doors and window-panes,
Life stirs in the gardens,
People snip at hedge and rosebush,
Birds sing.

THE RIGHT NOTE

THE FRIENDSHIP BOOK

SATURDAY — APRIL 12.

THERE'S a season for beginnings
When the world is fresh and new,
When we shape our dreams of all
The things we plan and hope to do.

A season for maturing
When we think and work and grow,
And a season for the harvesting of
All we've come to know.

And each successive season
Grows richer than the last,
As treasures of the present
Add to memories of the past.

Anon.

SUNDAY — APRIL 13.

LET every soul be subject unto the higher powers. For there is no power but of God: the powers that be are ordained of God.

Romans 13:1

MONDAY — APRIL 14.

THE American author James Fenimore Cooper, who told of his country's great forests and prairies in such books as "The Deerslayer" wrote:-
"Friendship that flows from the heart cannot be frozen by adversity."

Much has been written about friendship, but don't these words speak of the kind of friendship all of us would treasure, should we be fortunate enough to receive it? We should also be the willing givers of such friendship.

TUESDAY — APRIL 15.

WE all, at some time, make a decision that turns out to be a wrong one. The best thing is to go back and, where possible, aim for your goal another way. At such times I always remind myself of these wise words:

"Mistakes are painful when they happen, but years later a collection of mistakes is what is called experience."

Denis Waitley.

WEDNESDAY — APRIL 16.

I WONDER if you know these beautiful words from the 17th century? They come from a sermon which was preached at St Paul's in 1624 by John Donne, Dean of St Paul's, and make a wonderful thought for today — and all our tomorrows:

He brought light out of darkness, not out of a lesser light. He can bring thy Summer out of Winter, though thou have no Spring; though in the ways of fortune, or understanding, or conscience, thou have been denighted till now, wintered and frozen, clouded and eclipsed, damped and benumbed; smothered and stupefied till now, now God comes to thee, not as in the dawning of the day, not as in the bud of Spring, but as the sun at noon.

John Donne was born in London c.1573 and died in 1631. A poet and clergyman, he did not enter the church until he was forty-three years old.

THURSDAY — APRIL 17.

PROVERBS from around the world are an endless source of inspiration, like this Arabian one:

"He who has health, has hope,
And he who has hope, has everything."

FRIDAY — APRIL 18.

THE flower most associated with Easter is the daffodil. Unless Easter falls late in the calendar or the weather has been particularly warm, daffodils are usually at their best at this time, "fluttering and dancing in the breeze", and filling our churches with beauty.

The daffodil is the national emblem of Wales, worn by loyal Welsh people on St David's Day and there is a belief that whoever is lucky enough to discover the first bloom of the season will be blessed with more gold than silver.

Daffodil Sunday is celebrated on the first Sunday in April. It goes back to Victorian times when families would go out together, pick daffodils from their garden and take them to their local hospital to be given to the sick.

It is said that to dream of daffodils signifies love and happiness, and there can be few of us who are not made aware of the beauty of Easter time by the sight of golden daffodils in the sunshine:

Blossom and bud with Winter past,
joyfully have their fling,
And daffodils dancing along the path,
trumpet the news of Spring.

SATURDAY — APRIL 19.

SELDOM has there been a year when we have not had a robin in our garden, and one year we had the pleasure of a brood of small robin redbreasts, now long flown the nest.

I would miss our current resident robin, who often keeps me cheerful company when I venture outdoors. He's a bright-eyed little bird, ever hopeful of tasty tit-bits.

Robins are much-loved feathered friends all year round, and are especially associated with the great festivals of Christmas and Easter. Tradition says that on the first Good Friday when the robin tried to pull a thorn from the Crown Of Thorns it was stained by the blood of Christ.

He was a brave little bird, too, who flew to the aid of the tiny wren, when the wren flew to Hell to fetch fire for mankind, and returned to Earth with its feathers on fire. The bright breast of Robin Redbreast reminds us of that today.

SUNDAY — APRIL 20.

AND as they were afraid, and bowed down their faces to the earth, they said unto them, Why seek ye the living among the dead? He is not here, but is risen; remember how he spake unto you when he was yet in Galilee.

Luke 24:5-6

MONDAY — APRIL 21.

"LET yesterday be a lesson, today an action, and tomorrow a hope."

HEAVEN
SENT

TUESDAY — APRIL 22.

I WOULD like to share with you today these wise words which I take to heart each time I look in and say hello to Calum, a businessman who is never without a problem to solve. On his desk is a framed inscription which reads:

Worry does not empty tomorrow of its sorrow.
It merely empties today of its strength.

WEDNESDAY — APRIL 23.

THE sign of a good day is when, at its end, you can lean back and bask in the knowledge that you have completed your various tasks, knowing you've done as much as you can. In this context I am always reminded of this old proverb:

"Sow much, reap much. Sow little, reap little."

How rewarding it is to be at the "reaping" stage after a long day "sowing".

THURSDAY — APRIL 24.

HERE'S a pilgrim's prayer found in Ely Cathedral which I'd like to share with you today:

God of pilgrimage, be with me on
  my journey through this life;
Guard and defend me,
Shelter and feed me,
Challenge and inspire me,
Teach me and lead me,
And when my days are ended,
Welcome me home at last —
  To rest in your love for ever.

FRIDAY — APRIL 25.

I WAS at a very special birthday party when the guest of honour, Alice, a sprightly nonagenarian, gave us this advice for happiness:

"Have something to do, somebody to love, something to hope for."

Three simple essentials, she said, and so easy to remember. All three have stood the test of time — they work for everybody.

SATURDAY — APRIL 26.

FAITHFUL friends sustain us
When life's dark shadows fall —
Their words of hope encourage,
Make us feel ten feet tall.

Faithful friends are near us
When life is full of woe,
It's then they take us by the hand
To paths that we should go.

Faithful friends are with us
No matter where we roam
They come with the good Lord's blessing,
And lead us safely home.

Jenny Chaplin.

SUNDAY — APRIL 27.

IF we live in the Spirit, let us also walk in the Spirit.

Galatians 5:25

CAPITAL
CRESCENDO

FESTIVAL PIER

THE FRIENDSHIP BOOK

MONDAY — APRIL 28.

SOMEHOW, I think many people must feel like this at the end of a busy day . . . The routine of the workplace is behind them, and suddenly it feels good to start the journey into dreamland, picking up a favourite book and forgetting daily routine by dipping into a chapter or two.

As an old proverb says: "A book is like a garden carried in the pocket."

A garden is a delight, and many a quiet hour before midnight can be happily spent among the flowers of escapism and wisdom in this "paper garden".

TUESDAY — APRIL 29.

I HAVE no idea who originally said it, but I hope you'll agree that the following quotation is worth sharing:

"Do all the good you can in the world, and make as little noise about it as possible."

WEDNESDAY — APRIL 30.

A READER points out that while many people like to collect wise sayings, she herself collects humorous notices such as this one:

"On Saturday morning, the Ladies' Guild will hold their annual Jumble Sale. In collecting goods for this event, it is a splendid chance for all the ladies of the congregation to get rid of anything that is not worth keeping, but is too good to be thrown away. Don't forget to bring your husbands."

May

THURSDAY — MAY 1.

WE found Tom busy as usual in his potting shed surrounded by plant pots, bags of compost and packets of seeds. For such a big man, he was very gentle and handled the tiny, green shoots with great care.

"I have always tried to handle my marriage in the same way," he observed quietly when I remarked on his patience.

Creating a successful marriage or partnership requires skill and lots of tender, loving care. As with plants, love must be nurtured and kept in a sunny and cheerful situation. If left out in the cold, love will wither.

As Tom would tell you: "Look after what you have grown with T.L.C. You are the guardian of nature's precious and delicate plants."

FRIDAY — MAY 2.

MUCH has been written about habits, good and bad. An old friend has this quote on a plaque in his kitchen:

"A habit cannot be tossed out of the window; it must be coaxed down the stairs a step at a time."

How true! Getting rid of the bad habit is often a much harder task than acquiring a good one.

BUDS AND
BLOOMS

SATURDAY — MAY 3.

A TELEPHONE company gave advice to its customers about the best way of passing on unpleasant news. "Come straight to the point," it said, "but be prepared for a variety of reactions."

The way to pass on information like this is a question that taxes the resources of us all, especially if the news concerned directly affects a close friend.

One tip is "give a hug, or just a gentle hand on the arm". Another suggestion is to offer "companionable silence".

Isn't it comforting to know that, at the right moment tactful and reverential silence can mean so much, and speak, as it were, a thousand words of sympathy and true friendship.

SUNDAY — MAY 4.

A ND this is the will of him that sent me, that every one which seeth the Son, and believeth on him, may have everlasting life: and I will raise him up at the last day.

John 6:40

MONDAY — MAY 5.

E IGHT-year-old Lisa was chatting to her grandmother one day. Grandma told her, with a touch of pride, that she had been attending Bible Class for nearly fifty years.

Lisa looked at her sympathetically and patted her hand: "Don't worry about it, Grandma," she said, "maybe this year you will pass!"

TUESDAY — MAY 6.

VISTAS

*THE lush green of the valley, the blossom
  on the hill,
That drifts against the window, and sprays
  on window-sill.
The cool, refreshing raindrop, the sunset
  over the sea,
A vista of enchantment to spread tranquillity.
The fragrance of the flowers, their colours
  pastel bright,
And trees whose shadows alternate, in filtered
  pools of light.
A swan and its reflection, a sign of timeless grace,
A challenge to the rush of life's eternal race.
And as the day is closing, one star keeps vigil,
Till another dawn is breaking, through blossoms
  on the hill.*

Elizabeth Gozney.

WEDNESDAY — MAY 7.

UNTIL recent times it was common in the Scottish Highlands to leave one place empty at the table and I hope that there are houses where this custom is still observed to this day.

The thinking behind this idea was that you never knew when a stranger might come to the door in need of food and shelter and, in providing hospitality, Christ's words were fulfilled that whoever cared for someone hungry and thirsty cared also for Him.

THURSDAY — MAY 8.

ELLEN has always been a stalwart when it comes to helping out at church coffee mornings. She never brings home-made buns; she never makes jam or excels in sewing, but in the back room, at the kitchen sink, she is indispensable.

I asked her once if she didn't mind being left in charge of washing-up. "Francis," she said, "my cakes are awful and my biscuits are worse, but no-one has ever grumbled about the way I wash up. In any case," she added more seriously, "I may not be a good cook, but there's still something quite creative about transforming a heap of dirty dishes into a stack of shining crockery. And it's nice to feel that I'm playing my part."

I do admire Ellen. In my opinion, her good nature shines even more brightly than her clean china!

FRIDAY — MAY 9.

I LIKE the Spanish toast which says:
Health, love and money . . . and time to enjoy them!

Doesn't that say such a lot in a few words? After all, there can be few things more tragic than someone who, having worked hard to save for their Autumn years, does not in fact get time to enjoy a well-earned retirement.

So if you yourself have been granted the God-given gift of happy, healthy retirement days, then do remember to count your blessings.

SATURDAY — MAY 10.

"HAVE a good day!" The words have become time-worn with use, but it's the warm thought behind these words that matters. People wishing others a happy day is something never to be discouraged.

The value of a friendly greeting was well described by singer-actor W. F. Frame, who did charity work for his fellow-actors in Scotland early last century. Alongside his photograph he had posters outside theatres proclaiming:

"A warm hello, a cheerful shout
Is worth all the doctors round about."

That "cheerful shout", given spontaneously at the start of the day, can still bring inspiration.

SUNDAY — MAY 11.

AND Paul dwelt two whole years in his own hired house, and received all that came in unto him.

Acts 28:30

MONDAY — MAY 12.

ALLOW me to share with you today this thought from Johann Wolfgang von Goethe:

"The world is so empty if one thinks only of mountains, rivers and cities; but to know someone here and there who thinks and feels with us and though distant, is close to us in spirit, this makes the earth for us an inhabited garden."

Words to remember, I'm sure, when you think of trusted friends at home and abroad.

TUESDAY — MAY 13.

FRED, a neighbour, is a dog lover and an interested student of how they behave when living in our homes as "man's best friend".

We were talking about their various moods and habits when I asked him whether he thought our four-legged friends could teach their owners a useful tip or two for a happy lifestyle. I didn't have long to wait before Fred gave me his answer:

"No matter how often you face a setback, don't get too downhearted," he said. "Look at how your dog reacts; he doesn't pout when you scold him, but instead, romps right back to you within a minute. Then he wags his tail, stays happy and is friendly."

Wouldn't it be fine if we humans could be like our dogs, put on a happy face, stop harbouring those grudges, and "romp" right back when we suffer a setback?

WEDNESDAY — MAY 14.

THE night before Elizabeth was due to undergo a major operation she borrowed a pen from her nurse, cut a strip of sticking plaster and wrote on it: *"Not To Be Opened Before 8.30 a.m.!"*

Next morning the surgeon and his team just had to smile when their patient was wheeled into the operating theatre and they found the light-hearted notice.

It proves there's rarely an occasion when a smile isn't welcome!

<u>THURSDAY — MAY 15.</u>

O N her birthday a little girl asked her grandmother, "Why can't I always be as happy as I am today?"

Her grandmother replied, "Happiness isn't the end of the journey, it's all the signposts you see on your way. The ones that point to — A Friend In Need Of Help, Accepting A Challenge, Being Brave When Things Go Wrong, or Saying Something Cheerful To A Friend In Trouble.

"Every time you take the right turning you find the road to happiness, so be careful not to pass the signposts unnoticed."

I think she had the right idea about happiness.

<u>FRIDAY — MAY 16.</u>

M Y friend Bill enjoys singing of all kinds, including the robust sound of a male voice choir. At a church concert a group of men's voices delighted him and his wife Jane with some rousing choruses which included a selection from Haydn's oratorio "The Creation".

I once read that on first hearing this great work a leading authority of the day exclaimed, "To be able to write something so wonderful the composer must have been present at the very creation!"

This reminds us that to create great works of art, inspiration from above is needed. We should all be grateful that there are composers, artists and writers able to interpret such inspiration for our pleasure.

SATURDAY — MAY 17.

ANYONE travelling around West Yorkshire will be impressed by the lovely displays of flowers and attractive appearance of some road edges. They will catch sight of signs informing them that this is the work of The Groundwork Trust. Although it is a national organisation, it relies on dedicated local people in each area to carry out its work.

Frank Edwards was a railway inspector and was dismayed when he repeatedly saw the amount of rubbish strewn around and the desolation of many railway embankments and the ground nearby. After his retiral he decided to do something about improving the look of such areas and began working as a volunteer with The Groundwork Trust on projects to raise environmental standards.

This was some years ago and he organised teams of young people to help with the work. Some were from schools, some from the probation service and others from various environmental groups. When 74 years of age, Frank Edwards was awarded the MBE for his inspiration and dedication to The Groundwork Trust.

SUNDAY — MAY 18.

THEREFORE whosoever heareth these sayings of mine, and doeth them, I will liken him unto a wise man, which built his house upon a rock.

Matthew 7:24

MONDAY — MAY 19.

PAUL was surprised when a young man said he recalled him from years ago when they both lived on the same estate. Then the stranger said that he had always remembered the advice Paul had given him; it was that, whatever the circumstances, you could achieve an ambition if you tried hard enough.

The young man had suffered serious injuries in a car accident and had been confined to a wheelchair for many months, but he remembered those words. He was happy to say that he had gone on to achieve success as an athlete — all because he was convinced by the advice he'd received. The strange thing was that Paul could not remember saying these words but was glad to be reminded of them because, having been made redundant, he was going through a difficult time himself.

Sometimes your own words return to you in the most unexpected way!

TUESDAY — MAY 20.

HERE are two thoughts from the 19th-century writer and thinker Sydney Smith for you to share today:

"Whatever you are by nature, keep to it; never desert your line of talent. Be what nature intended you for, and you will succeed."

"The greatest of all mistakes is to do nothing if you think you can only do a little. Go ahead and do what you can."

WEDNESDAY — MAY 21.

I HAD so many problems,
  The worries crowding in,
I used to toss and turn at night,
  Just where could I begin?
And no-one seemed to know or care,
  Or help with any task,
Until the day I heard God's voice:
  "You only need to ask."

I felt ashamed and made a vow
  To start each day in prayer,
The problems didn't disappear,
  But help was always there.
Whatever life may bring your way,
  Whatever work or task,
Your God will help and understand,
  You only need to ask.

Iris Hesselden.

THURSDAY — MAY 22.

MY friend Jonathan told me that one day he was standing in the central concourse of a city train station, watching the scene as commuters dashed to their various platforms, some catching, others missing, their connections. One crestfallen traveller turned to him and remarked:

"You never realise the value of sixty vital seconds until you become someone who has missed his train."

Words for all of us to keep in mind!

FRIDAY — MAY 23.

"WHAT are you studying so intently, Francis?" asked the Lady of the House one day, as she walked out into the garden. I turned round from my comfortable seat, feeling a little guilty, as I was meant to be weeding.

"I was just remembering my painting lessons many years ago," I told her. She sat down beside me and I asked her to look carefully at the plants and trees, then tell me what she saw. "Many different shades of green," she replied.

"Exactly!" I said.

What I had remembered was being taught never to use a ready-mixed green. It had seemed a nuisance then, but makes perfect sense now. The more you look at trees, the more colours and shades you will see.

It's a bit like life really, isn't it? The more details we observe, the more we learn and the more fascinating everything becomes. Now, perhaps my painting lessons weren't such a waste of time after all!

SATURDAY — MAY 24.

EVERY partnership, I know you will agree, has to accept its quota of minor huffs and the world realises that little disputes are to be expected from time to time in nearly every home.

I think that such sporadic differences are clearly summed up by these lines which I read one day:

"Love is being able to walk arm-in-arm —
Even when you don't see eye-to-eye."

SUNDAY — MAY 25.

BUT if the Spirit of him that raised up Jesus from the dead dwell in you, he that raised up Christ from the dead shall also quicken your mortal bodies by his Spirit that dwelleth in you.

Romans 8:11

MONDAY — MAY 26.

AN earnest-looking author once sat writing in his quiet study in a small building near Oulton Broad in Suffolk. His life at that time was peaceful, but in days gone by it had been eventful. In fact, he'd had many adventures while working as a Bible translator in Russia and Spain.

At Oulton, George Borrows remembered that as a boy he had aimed at success and he had achieved this, in spite of many career ups and downs. His task now was to encourage other people to realise what determination and ambition could achieve and in one of his books "Lavengro" he wrote:

"Let but the will of a human being be turned to one particular object and it is ten to one, that sooner or later, he achieves it."

TUESDAY — MAY 27.

WILLIAM, a hotelier friend, often quotes his grandmother's favourite sayings, one of which is: "It'll not be long till a wee while."

Perhaps another way of telling us all that by being patient, eventually everything comes to those who wait?

WEED LIKE TO
SAY HELLO

WEDNESDAY — MAY 28.

HERE'S a question for you to consider today: What is the prescription that needs no medicine, the weight control plan where you don't have to diet, the exercise that needs no gymnasium?

You've guessed already, of course! It's something that costs not a single penny and which is readily available. Try a walk wherever you find yourself, in the good, clean, fresh air.

THURSDAY — MAY 29.

WHICH days deserve to be earmarked and remembered for months, even years to come? Sometimes such days can be in the height of Summer, or during a special holiday. Or maybe they come during the joys of the festive season — a get-together for Christmas or New Year.

We all have our own favourite days to remember, ones we circle in the diary of our minds for now and all time. Yet ordinary days should not be discounted either. The writer Lucy Montgomery summed it up neatly:

"The nicest and sweetest days are not those on which anything very splendid or wonderful or exciting happens, but just those that bring simple little pleasures, following one another softly, like pearls slipping off a string."

Now, wouldn't it be splendid if today should prove to have been one of these special days for you? Remember, you've got all of 365 to choose from. And 366 in every Leap Year!

FRIDAY — MAY 30.

NO matter your circumstances, you need never feel lonely. Take Kate, for example, in her seventies and living alone. She saw a car-boot sale advertised, and decided to go along.

Once there, she bought herself a big bag of brightly-coloured knitting wool oddments. Kate decided to knit blanket squares, and soon she had an attractive rainbow collection completed. She mentioned this to someone in a local shop.

"And now you've the fun of joining them up," said her listener.

"Well, actually," Kate replied, "it's the joining up I'm not too keen on — it's rather tedious."

As a result of their chat the two ladies, once strangers, started to meet up regularly with Kate knitting, and Helen, her new friend, doing the job she particularly liked — sewing.

Together the pair made a fine team, and many a happy afternoon they spent together.

SATURDAY — MAY 31.

A FRIEND back from working amongst the poor in Brazil tells me the most inspiring thing he saw was near a huge rubbish dump on the edge of a city.

"Thousands of people scavenged there," he told me, "but beside it was a small garden, fenced off, where some of them were growing vegetables to eat."

A tiny patch, but a symbol of hope and courage in the midst of poverty.

June

THEREFORE, my beloved brethren, be ye stedfast, unmoveable, always abounding in the work of the Lord, forasmuch as ye know that your labour is not in vain in the Lord.

Corinthians I 15:58

THE DOVE-COTE

I KNOW an old cottage with silvery thatch,
And a door that is always on the latch,
A garden, where blue delphiniums vie
With the deep hue of the Summer sky,
And there, a delight for one and all,
A dove-cote stands, by the grey stone wall,
Alive with the soft, sweet murmurings
Of cooing doves, and the whirr of wings.

As white as the foam on a sunlit sea,
Or blossom that gleams on a hawthorn tree,
Or pure white paint, that is fresh and new,
Or the whitest daisy that ever grew,
With their ruby eyes, these fluttering birds
Are almost too beautiful for words,
And it's easy to see why the gentle dove
Is a symbol of harmony, peace, and love.

Kathleen O'Farrell.

TUESDAY — JUNE 3.

SOMETIMES the older ones amongst us can teach the young a thing or two!

When the Children's Society organised a fund-raising sponsored walk "Across Worcester", it was allowed to be interpreted fairly liberally. Consequently, as well as going by foot, it was done by bicycle, by water and even by donkey.

However, it was the hardy female residents of Bedwardine Rest Home who impressed everybody when they zipped into action with zimmer frames. They crossed the grounds of the home at a fine pace, raising £150 for the Children's Society.

As a result the Society's Worcester branch decided that a large colour television which had been donated by British Telecom, the sponsors, should be presented to the residents of Bedwardine House. A tangible reminder of what can be achieved if we really put our minds to it!

WEDNESDAY — JUNE 4.

MY friend Erik, who lives in Stockholm, tells me the latest news from his family and he mentions from time to time Sweden's folklore. I want to share with you this old Swedish proverb:

"Fear less, hope more,
Eat less, chew more,
Whine less, breathe more,
Talk less, say more,
Hate less, love more —
Do this, and all things good
will be with you and yours."

THURSDAY — JUNE 5.

I READ a touching story one day, told by a caring mother. Her daughter, who had left home, was going through a stressful time at work.

One day, the daughter had gone to her mother's house, made herself a cup of tea, then helped herself to a generous spray of expensive perfume. Later she rang to apologise, saying, "I was in such a state — I just needed a whiff of my mum; it always makes me feel better!"

What a comfort a mother is! Even a "whiff" of one makes you feel good. By the way, when the daughter went back-packing around Australia, her mother discovered a discarded shirt and found consolation for the separation by picking it up and hugging it.

There's the meaning of true love when a simple suggestion, a mere whiff, can bring two hearts closer together.

FRIDAY — JUNE 6.

MY WORD

A FRIENDLY word can do a lot
To ease a situation,
Where circumstances can be thought
To fashion aggravation.

If ever any token
Of disappointment lurks,
When a friendly word is spoken,
My word, it often works.
J. M. Robertson.

THE FRIENDSHIP BOOK

I HAVE always been impressed by the power of words, especially when expressed in fine poetry. I was not surprised to read that Terry Waite, in his long months of solitary confinement, while a prisoner in the Middle East, found consolation in repeating to himself great verse, as well as prayers. He fell back on memory to find pleasure in the expression of fine language.

In his own words: "The harmony of language helped me find some form of inner structure and that enabled me to keep hold of inner identity when it appeared that my body as such was failing." As we know, the body and spirit of this brave man did not fail in spite of suffering and privation.

A fine example to the rest of us to seek encouragement and strength in the works of great literature.

SUNDAY — JUNE 8.

GRACE be with all them that love our Lord Jesus Christ in sincerity. Amen.

Ephesians 6:24

MONDAY — JUNE 9.

A READER from Ireland recently sent me a copy of her favourite toast:

"May you ever travel new pathways, explore distant horizons and at the end of life's journey, come safely back home."

TUESDAY — JUNE 10.

TAMARA was a teenager in an orphanage in Moldavia — a little-known part of eastern Europe.

She had experienced a very difficult childhood, and when welfare workers visited, it was discovered that young Tamara had never been accustomed to sweets, toys or any of the other things which more fortunate youngsters in other parts of the world take for granted.

But what moved the visiting welfare workers more than anything else was the fact that when Tamara was given a bag of sweets, she divided the contents among those unable to get out of bed, and didn't keep a single sweet for herself.

Despite her own needs, Tamara displayed a spirit of generosity which put the well-being of all the other children first — and in so doing gave herself the kind of quiet contentment which comes only from placing the needs of others above one's own.

WEDNESDAY — JUNE 11.

"A GARDEN is a lovesome thing," wrote the poet T. E. Brown, while Dorothy Gurney, another poet, said, "One is nearer God's heart in a garden than anywhere else on earth."

The writer Francis Bacon put it well in five words when he described gardens as "the purest of human pleasures".

All worth remembering when your back is aching and your hands blistered!

WHEELY
DELIGHTFUL

THE FRIENDSHIP BOOK

<u>THURSDAY — JUNE 12.</u>

BETHANY, who is ten years young, gave us all something to think about when she joined her family for a drive in the country. They were passing through lots of small villages and everywhere people seemed to be smiling and waving to them. Suddenly her parents realised why this was happening.

"I do this even on our school bus," Bethany confided. "You see, I've discovered that every time I wave to people, they stop what they're doing and wave back."

Now, isn't that a wonderful idea for us all? Just show a bit of outgoing friendliness, and the world will smile back at you.

<u>FRIDAY — JUNE 13.</u>

A VERY popular TV programme asked "Who Wants To Be A Millionaire?" The contestant was given four possible answers to each question and had to give the correct one in order to move up a stage. As the questions got more difficult, he or she could use one of their lifelines and ask the audience to help out, or phone a friend who would be likely to know the answer.

What a blessing our own lifelines are — the phone which rings just when we feel in need of cheering up, the unexpected bunch of flowers or the invitation to "come and share our tea because we know this hasn't been a good day for you."

It's good to be on the receiving end — and rewarding to be the giver.

SATURDAY — JUNE 14.

MY friend Ken, who is a librarian, had an enquiry regarding the lines inscribed on the base of the Statue Of Liberty. He later drew my attention to the welcome which the New World set out to give to those seeking to escape the Old World:

Give me your tired, your poor,
Your huddled masses yearning to be free;
The wretched refuse of your teeming shore,
Send these, the homeless, tempest-tossed, to me;
I lift my lamp beside the golden door!

These lines are from a sonnet by Emma Lazarus who died in 1887 before she was 40 years old, but whose immortal lines on the Statue Of Liberty are engraved for all to see.

SUNDAY — JUNE 15.

THOU art worthy, O Lord, to receive glory and honour and power: for thou hast created all things, and for thy pleasure they are and were created.

Revelation 4:11

MONDAY — JUNE 16.

MEMORY plays an important part in the lives of all of us today, be it sharp or blunt, good or, sadly, slowly losing its former strength. That is why I want to offer you today these words of the poet Christina Rossetti:

Better by far you should forget and smile,
Than that you should remember and be sad.

TUESDAY — JUNE 17.

JENNY and Pauline were teenage members of a Christian youth fellowship in Surrey. They had never known their respective grandmothers, so when their minister challenged them to "adopt a granny", they readily accepted.

The elderly lady they chose to "adopt" couldn't remember when she had last had a young visitor. Pauline and Jenny began to visit her every week, doing small jobs such as dusting and weeding. And although their adopted granny wasn't very mobile, they patiently walked with her to the end of her garden and back to the house.

This went on week after week until eventually the old lady was taken into hospital where, sadly, she later died. The girls' visits were never mentioned in the local paper, and most people did not know about them.

But for one lonely old lady, those visits and the selfless concern of two teenage girls were priceless. It showed that someone cared, and gave her renewed hope.

WEDNESDAY — JUNE 18.

WE live in an age of rush and bustle. Now and again I like to remind myself of some words by Ralph Emerson, the American philosopher. He pointed out: "Nature never hurries; atom by atom, little by little, she achieves her work."

Take it easy, take Nature's pace. You will get there just the same!

THE FRIENDSHIP BOOK

I OFTEN wonder how anyone can be bored in a world that is full of beauty, charm and adventure, so may I suggest that you tackle something new and different sometime soon? Fresh experiences keep us young at heart and full of fun, so why not just go for a leisurely walk, or if it's raining take a stroll and watch the world go by in a busy shopping mall?

As Jawaharlal Nehru said: "There is no end to the adventures that we can have if only we seek them with our eyes open."

THE Lady of the House and I had been to a most enjoyable concert. It was held in a village hall, and was an entirely amateur affair, the product of local talent and enthusiasm.

On the way home the Lady of the House was in a thoughtful mood. "You know, Francis," she mused, "if only we could organise life just as if we were putting on a show, it might be a very good thing."

She continued, "If only we could always be prepared to give so readily of our own special gifts, working together towards a common goal, each striving to play our part, whether as star performer, scenery painter, or simply giving applause and encouragement — who knows what wonderful things we might manage to produce?"

Now that's a theory that really does deserve a standing ovation!

SATURDAY — JUNE 21.

HOW often have you heard the phrase: "I could write a book . . . if only I had the time!" Well, my answer to that is try to make the time, for just like a true friend, time is on your side.

After all, if Scotswoman Janet Hamilton, the 19th-century Langloan Poet, could write books and reams of emotive poetry while bringing up a family of 10 in poor circumstances — and she also had to cope with her own blindness in later life — what is there to stop you?

Something else is worth mentioning. Although Janet Hamilton could read, she had never attended school and was unable to write until she reached the age of 50.

Talk about making time for the important things in life . . .

SUNDAY — JUNE 22.

AND all the people came early in the morning to him in the temple, for to hear him.

Luke 21:38

MONDAY — JUNE 23.

THE Lady of the House gave a gentle smile and a knowing nod when we came on this notice outside a tiny village church recently:

"Grant me, please, the ability to start to like all the people I have never liked, and the good fortune to appreciate the hundreds that I already do."

TUESDAY — JUNE 24.
SPECIAL BIRTHDAY

SEVENTY — I don't believe it!
Did someone change the date?
It doesn't seem so very long
Since I was forty-eight.
What happened to my fifties?
They simply slipped away,
Then suddenly came sixty —
Another special day.

When I see the lines and wrinkles
I know it must be true,
And yet I'm twenty-one inside
With many things to do.
I'd like to be one hundred,
Feeling hale and hearty,
So make a date, in thirty years
You're welcome to my party!

Iris Hesselden.

WEDNESDAY — JUNE 25.

A FRIEND told me that once, when she was living in Hong Kong, she attended an Autumn Moon Festival. On the first night the moon was welcomed and on the second, when it was full, people held a huge party and there were great celebrations. On the third and last night, they bade the moon farewell.

Impressed with the sincerity of all those taking part, my friend says she will never again take the moon and its beauty for granted.

CHAPTER
AND
VERSE

THURSDAY — JUNE 26.

I WONDER if you have heard the story of the young man and the starfish. One day, at early dawn, he was seen walking along the beach picking up stranded starfish and throwing them back into the receding sea. On being asked why he was doing this, he said that if he didn't, once the sun came up the stranded starfish would die.

"But the beach stretches for miles, and there must be thousands of stranded starfish," remarked an onlooker. "What difference can you make?"

The young man looked at the starfish in his hand, and threw it to safety into the water. "It makes a difference to this one," he replied.

We have so many worthwhile causes asking for our support these days that we might sometimes wonder if our small donations of money and time can really help. Well, remember that young man and the starfish, and then your doubts will surely disappear. And, if you pass on this story, then just think of the chain reaction you might set up!

FRIDAY — JUNE 27.

DONALD was facing going away to live in the town for several years and he dreaded leaving behind all that he loved in the countryside — the woods, the hills and the river.

One evening, only days before he was due to leave, he was sitting grumbling to a friend about his reluctance to depart. She took his hand and smiled and said, "You have to let the people become the grass of the city!"

SATURDAY — JUNE 28.

SARAH HINTON, a 15-year-old schoolgirl, was asked to list the attributes that make "a friend". She wrote:

A friend is someone who is there no matter what!
Someone who gives advice, NOT tells you what to do!
A friend is a shoulder to lean on, a hand to hold.
A friend doesn't have to look or act or dress a certain way.
The only thing that matters is what's on the inside.

May all our friends be like Sarah's friends.

SUNDAY — JUNE 29.

I HAVE glorified thee on the earth: I have finished the work which thou gavest me to do. And now; O Father, glorify thou me with thine own self with the glory which I had with thee before the world was.

John 17:4-5

MONDAY — JUNE 30.

DO you get depressed when you see graffiti? Believe it or not, archaeologists discovered scrawled across a wall in one of the ancient parts of Cairo the words "What's the point of it all?"

It's a comfort to know that we haven't changed much and that being frustrated by life is no new phenomenon. It's good to remember, too, that there is a point to it all, and that life is very much worth living.

July

O H, butterfly on folded wings
Alighting on my hand,
So delicate a graceful form,
I think you understand
My eagerness to be your friend,
By talking to you now,
And watching as you hover by
The blossom, mid the bough.
Though limited your freedom's span,
I hope you'll live to see
Another day of freedom's joy,
And still remember me.

Elizabeth Gozney.

ONE day, I had stepped off the bus and was walking away when a young lad rushed towards the vehicle shouting, "Stop! Stop!" But it was too late — the bus was already moving off and no amount of shouting could stop it.

"Hard luck," I said. "If you'd run a bit faster you might have made it."

"I ran fast enough, at least as fast as I could," he puffed. "I just didn't start soon enough."

Mind you don't "miss the bus" today!

<u>THURSDAY — JULY 3.</u>

O LD Sam's garden is always so neat and brimming with colour, but one day as I passed I noticed him straighten up somewhat painfully. "Why don't you save yourself work and pave over some of your borders?" I suggested.

"Francis, as long as there's a working bone in my body, I'll carry on," he replied. "Will I tell you why?" I nodded.

"Well, one morning as I waited in the pension queue I overheard a woman telling a friend how much she loved to look at other people's front gardens as she passed through the village. 'I can't go to flower shows these days,' she'd added, 'the walking is too much for me now, but I can see these local gardens in all their glory'."

Sam's garden continues to bloom beautifully from season to season, and doubtless will do so for many years. He certainly taught me a lesson that day about the things in life that can give pleasure to others.

Come to think of it, perhaps it's time I renewed our flowering plants on the window-sill, for they're beginning to look past their best!

<u>FRIDAY — JULY 4.</u>

T HE Spanish writer Baltasar Gracian wrote these words in the 17th century:

"Friendship multiplies the good of life and divides the evil . . ." What a lovely turn of phrase, one which makes a delightful thought for today, and all the world's tomorrows.

SATURDAY — JULY 5.

WHEN visiting churches I often find encouraging literature set out for the benefit of visitors. You might look on it as a sort of church advertising, trying to attract "customers"! One day I picked up a leaflet in a Yorkshire church on which were printed some memorable words from Mother Teresa of Calcutta:

"Be kind and merciful. Let no one ever come to you without coming away better and happier. Be the living expression of God's kindness: kindness in your face, kindness in your eyes, kindness in your warm greeting. To everybody give always a happy smile — give them not only your smile but your heart!"

I think a church whose members try to live up to such high ideals deserves to grow, don't you?

SUNDAY — JULY 6.

AND a certain scribe came, and said unto him, Master, I will follow thee whithersoever thou goest.
                                                    Matthew 8:19

MONDAY — JULY 7.

CHILDREN can often take things so literally, can't they? One afternoon, when asked to pop next door and ask how old Mrs Barton was, young Jane came back with these words:

"Mrs Barton says it's a lady's privilege not to disclose her age. But, if you *must* know, she'll be eighty-three in November."

TUESDAY — JULY 8.

THE Lady of the House was asked to forward a recipe to a friend, so she happily sat down to write out the instructions. After she had listed the necessary ingredients, she came to the part that advised, "Stir occasionally", but she suddenly wasn't sure if it had two c's or two s's.

Rather than risk being regarded as a careless speller, she jotted down "stir now and then". Isn't that a bit like life, really? Whatever the problem happens to be, there's usually an acceptable way round it.

WEDNESDAY — JULY 9.

IF someone makes you joyful
Then go ahead and share it,
And if it brings an extra smile
I'm sure that you can spare it.
When there's a disappointment,
Don't worry, never mind it,
There's so much beauty in the world,
Just look around and find it.

When there's good news around you
Don't be afraid to shout it,
For many times our dreams come true
So never, ever doubt it.
If you have love within you
Don't keep it, always give it,
This life is ours to celebrate,
So go ahead and live it!

Iris Hesselden.

THURSDAY — JULY 10.

*T*HE *S.S. Friendship sails the sea*
*   of life, and hopes to steer*
A steady course, where there may be
*   Horizons bright and clear.*
It's always keen to have on board
*   A willing entourage,*
Aware of storms, but can afford
*   To shout, "Bon Voyage!"*

J. M. Robertson.

FRIDAY — JULY 11.

THE two elderly gentlemen in the supermarket queue shook hands warmly with each other, obviously pleased at the meeting. What appeared to me to be equally obvious, was that neither had a lot of time to stand and chat.

From the snatches of conversation I happened to hear, their days were fully occupied. "Do you remember," one asked his friend, "how we were told that life begins at 40?"

"I know what you're going to say," came the reply. "It really begins when you retire!"

They both laughed and compared notes about the meetings they had to attend and the people they needed to see. How marvellous, I thought, to lead such busy and useful lives.

We have no need to fear retirement. If we are active and interested in others' well-being, there is much we can do to be of service. May they — and all of us — have many busy, happy years ahead!

SATURDAY — JULY 12.

WHEN Sir Edward Elgar was a young man, a friend overheard him trying out a new melody on the piano.

"What's that, Edward?" he asked.

"I don't know yet," was the reply, "but something might be made from it."

"Well, I shouldn't give up the day job," was his friend's advice.

However, Elgar worked at the music and eventually it became one of the most well-loved parts of his Enigma Variations — Nimrod.

So today remember all those like Sir Edward Elgar who, faced with a problem, worked at it and "made something of it".

SUNDAY — JULY 13.

NOW the God of peace be with you all. Amen.
Romans 15:33

MONDAY — JULY 14.

THE name of the Gorbals in Glasgow is known worldwide. But perhaps not so well known is the fact that some forty years ago, in that same district of Glasgow lived a woman who was known locally as "The Angel Of The Gorbals".

Having herself once been crippled, before faith-healing miraculously cured her, Margaret Gilmour then spent six years of her life as a devoted friend to the elderly, disabled and housebound.

Many a lonely person had cause to be grateful for gifts and, above all, the hand of friendship.

MIX AND
MATCH

TUESDAY — JULY 15.

HERE is a thought for today from the prolific pen of Anon:

"Of all God's gifts to men laughter is one of the most subtle, and is one of the most precious. It has neither nationality nor religion. As an equaliser, it has no equal . . ."

How true, but let it be kind and friendly laughter at no-one's expense — now, that surely, is the best laughter of all!

WEDNESDAY — JULY 16.

BERT, a retired builder, loves his garden, and can usually be found there, working hard, nurturing plants, sowing seeds and generally planning horticultural matters for the future. As gardening rarely yields instant results, I once complimented him on his unflagging faith that his hard work would pay off.

He scratched his head thoughtfully. "Well, yes," he agreed, "but then I always think that the faith of gardeners is nothing when compared to that of the builders who laboured on the great cathedrals such as Durham or Canterbury. In those days the work often took centuries to complete, and many of the men who toiled there must have known they would never see the finished results. Yet still they worked on, sure that their efforts would be pleasing to God."

All work done to enhance this world must surely be pleasing to Him, whether in stone or in flowers.

THE FRIENDSHIP BOOK

<u>THURSDAY — JULY 17.</u>

WHEN you think of the many inventions which have transformed our lives, the camera quickly comes to mind. Nearly all of us have one and we treasure snapshots of family and friends.

The very first camera was a little cardboard box with a small hole pierced through the side and specially-treated paper inserted inside. It was discovered that when the box was positioned with the hole facing an object, in time the light projecting through the hole would create an image on the paper.

From those humble beginnings the camera as we know it today was created, and what pleasure it has given all of us! We can effortlessly capture important events like holidays, birthdays and anniversaries.

Photographs will always be a special moment in time captured forever. Just think, modern photography began with a humble little cardboard box all those years ago.

<u>FRIDAY — JULY 18.</u>

I'M sure you will have noticed how people can often be divided into two categories — the quiet ones and those who are always talking non-stop, airing their favourite ideas and notions.

An old American proverb leaves us with food for thought when it says:

"Listen, or your tongue will make you deaf."

Words worth keeping in mind.

SATURDAY — JULY 19.

A S a member of a forceful, often somewhat argumentative, village hall committee, Sue had been through a testing year, so I was surprised to find her beaming when I bumped into her on her way home from the AGM.

"I've had such a nice compliment, Francis," she said happily. "During the meeting, when they thanked the chairman, treasurer and secretary for all their hard work, they added an extra vote of gratitude. They said they also wanted to thank the peacemaker — and they meant *me!*"

I was so pleased for Sue, for all too often the quiet work of those who do their best to reconcile differences is not acknowledged.

But as someone much wiser than me said long ago: "Blessed are the peacemakers: for they shall be called the children of God."

SUNDAY — JULY 20.

I WILL call on the Lord, who is worthy to be praised: so shall I be saved from mine enemies.

Samuel II 22:4

MONDAY — JULY 21.

W E all get a bit cross at times, even though we know it's the wrong thing to do. As long ago as 170 A.D. Marcus Aurelius pointed out that the rages people get into often do more harm than whatever annoyed them.

Here is a thought to help keep you calm: "a temper lost is a chance lost".

TUESDAY — JULY 22.

HERE'S a quotation by the writer Frederick E. Crane who, I am sure, got it 100 per cent. right when he said:

"To make a man happy, fill his hands with work, his heart with affection, his mind with purpose, his memory with useful knowledge, and his future with hope."

WEDNESDAY — JULY 23.

"**I** LOVE those television programmes about exploring!" enthused one of our neighbours, looking at his watch in anticipation of a favourite show.

"Well, don't let me detain you," I answered across the fence, and off he went with a cheery wave and a smile.

I sat a little longer in the garden, lost in my own thoughts as the sun sank below the horizon. Man has accomplished so much through the years, discovering remote areas of the world and even landing on the moon. There will always be intrepid explorers and adventurers but for many of us, perhaps our own corner of the universe holds sufficient wonder. As I went indoors later, I remembered something I'd once read, written by T. S. Eliot:

"We shall not cease from exploration, and the end of all our exploring will be to arrive where we started and know the place for the first time."

Isn't it true there is so much to explore around us — and also within us?

THURSDAY — JULY 24.

IN church one Sunday the congregation started the service with a modern hymn which many of us like very much:

Father, I place into your hands
The things that I can't do.
Father, I place into your hands
The times that I've been through.
Father, I place into your hands
The way that I should go,
For I know I always can trust you.

It continues with our concerns for our families and friends, the things that trouble us and the many things we have to be thankful for — all to be entrusted into the hands of God.

What better way to start any day?

FRIDAY — JULY 25.

A VISIT to the home where John, Charles and other members of the Wesley family lived is a memorable experience. For many years now, Epworth Old Rectory has been open to visitors.

The present house gives many glimpses into the Wesleys' home life. For example, upstairs can be seen letters which Rev. Samuel Wesley wrote, including one to the Archbishop of York. "I'm so full of God's mercies that neither my heart nor eyes can hold them," he said.

To read about the homes of famous people is interesting enough, but to actually visit them can be an uplifting and enlightening experience.

SATURDAY — JULY 26.

A NON-CHRISTIAN recently asked why the Lord's Prayer was said so regularly in Christian church services. The first, and most obvious, reply given was — because it was taught to us by Jesus Christ himself.

Quite true, but surely there is more to it than that. Why has it lived — word for word — for centuries? Was it just blind obedience? Was it superstition, as the questioner had hinted? Read or recite it slowly and see if you can spot the answer.

Isn't it simple when you reflect?

Nowhere in the prayer do the words "I" or "my" or "me" occur. Throughout every plea in the Prayer we are led to think of others. And that is the power of this amazing, enduring prayer.

SUNDAY — JULY 27.

J ESUS saith unto her, Said I not unto thee, that, if thou wouldest believe, thou shouldest see the glory of God?

John 11:40

MONDAY — JULY 28.

"W HEN ill befalls, a friend's kind eye beams comfort."

This is a favourite quotation both of the Lady of the House and myself. Written by Euripides, the great Athenian poet and playwright, it is as true today as when it was written, four hundred and eight years before the birth of Christ.

MEADOW
SWEET

TUESDAY — JULY 29.

LET me share with you today these words by Sir James Dewar, the famous scientist, who was born in 1877: "Minds are like parachutes. They only function when they are open."

WEDNESDAY — JULY 30.

THE Lady of the House has a friend, Jenny, who was once presented to Princess Diana, Duchess Of Rothesay, on the lovely Island of Bute in Scotland. She has a framed photograph of the happy occasion on her sideboard.

Discussing the event Jenny pointed out that what she remembers most is Diana's care and compassion for the elderly. It seems that farther down the receiving line an old lady, nervous at the fast approaching Royal handshake, dropped her walking-stick with a resounding clank.

And from all the people there on that crowded quayside, it was Diana who went out of her way, bent down and then returned the stick with a beaming smile.

A small act of courtesy, perhaps, but it says a great deal. And doesn't it leave a lovely warm feeling at the memory?

THURSDAY — JULY 31.

STEP out boldly on the road
And combat gloom with all your might;
Help others with a heavier load,
For those in darkness — be their light.
                                Earle Douglas.

August

FRIDAY — AUGUST 1.

I WONDER how often an apparently ordinary service in a little village church is enlivened by something out of the ordinary as in this tale.

One Sunday, the preacher had reached the end of his sermon, and announced the final hymn, a most appropriate one for a lovely warm Summer evening:

"All things praise Thee, Lord most high . . ."

Then as the organist struck up the tune, the worshippers in the pews were joined by half a dozen visitors — six beautiful Red Admiral butterflies, which fluttered delicately around the sanctuary, one settling on the pulpit Bible as if to reinforce the message of the hymn.

An everyday service, made especially memorable by the presence of the winged visitors, which are apparently much more at home amid stinging nettles.

SATURDAY — AUGUST 2.

I LIKE these words from the writer Jack Kornfield:

"When we get too caught up in the busyness of the world, we lose connection with one another — and with ourselves."

SUNDAY — AUGUST 3.

THERE is none holy as the Lord: for there is none beside thee: neither is there any rock like our God.

Samuel I 2:2

MONDAY — AUGUST 4.

HENRY Wadsworth Longfellow, the 19th-century poet, was an eminent professor of modern languages at Harvard University and became so popular in the United Kingdom and indeed, throughout the English-speaking world, that today there is a monument to him in Westminster Abbey.

His writings cover many aspects of life and living, but one of his best is surely this telling little gem on the subject of friendship:

"Ah, how good it feels! The hand of an old friend."

Firm and true, that strong clasp, in times good as well as bad, means so much.

TUESDAY — AUGUST 5.

IT was a wet August afternoon on the seafront. Disgruntled holidaymakers were bemoaning the sudden downpour.

Then the words of a happily-skipping-along toddler brought sunshine into the hearts of all who were lucky enough to catch them:

"Granny, don't worry! God made the rain as well, didn't He?"

THE FRIENDSHIP BOOK

<u>WEDNESDAY — AUGUST 6.</u>

WE received a cheerful letter recently from a friend who lives 5000 miles distant, telling of a new plan in her life. "I have decided," Freda wrote, "to make something of every minute. I have decided to sing my song, dance while I can, and celebrate life. It enriches the soul. Doing less is an injustice to whatever gifts we have been given."

Then she added, "Tomorrow is now."

The Lady of the House and I are listening to our faraway friend's advice, celebrating life's gifts today. Perhaps you'd like to do the same.

<u>THURSDAY — AUGUST 7.</u>

WHAT a precious gift of life
This tiny baby boy,
A helpless mite who's just arrived
To fill our days with joy.
A button nose, a rosebud mouth
And trusting eyes of blue,
Our hearts are overwhelmed with love
As we just look at you.

Lost in wonderment and awe
Enraptured with delight,
We gaze upon your sleeping form
All tucked up for the night.
One of the mysteries of life
The miracle of birth,
It seems an angel's brought a touch
Of heaven down to earth.

Kathleen Gillum.

FRIDAY — AUGUST 8.

THE Lady of the House could hardly wait to tell me about Caroline, a family friend who had recently relocated to Britain after many years of living abroad.

It seems that when Caroline left behind all her Spanish friends, rather than say a tearful and final-sounding "goodbye", she gave each one a small gift, together with a card on which she had written these emotive words:

Good friends never say goodbye — they simply say, "See you soon."

A lovely thought, don't you agree?

SATURDAY — AUGUST 9.

I LOVE walking in our local park, for it's always full of colour and interest. Often I pause to chat with the gardener in charge, and I once asked him what was his favourite sort of plant.

He scratched his head thoughtfully. "Trees," he said at last, "for much as I like the shrubs and flowers, there's a kind of continuity about trees. I know that many of the trees I enjoy today were planted by men who lived long ago, just as I know that the trees I plant will be appreciated by generations as yet unborn.

"And I hope that one day, they, too, in their turn, will do some planting. A tree is our gift to the future."

A wonderful gift indeed, that brings pleasure to so many!

THE FRIENDSHIP BOOK

THEN Peter and the other apostles answered and said, We ought to obey God rather than men.

Acts 5:29

MONDAY — AUGUST 11.

THANK You, Lord, for the gift of friends,
Their comfort, help and care,
For all the joy and happiness,
The special things we share.
Thank You for those other times,
The days of long ago,
The memories, and hopes and dreams
That only they can know.

Thank You for the helping hands
When problems crowd around,
For all the patient listening
The kindness I have found.
For all the steadfast loyalty
On which my trust depends,
Let me repay this love today,
And thank You, Lord, for friends.

Iris Hesselden.

TUESDAY — AUGUST 12.

OFTEN it is an innocent remark in an unlikely setting which can make us smile. Take the intimation given by a minister of mature years:

"The collection today will be towards the fund for getting rid of dry rot in the pulpit."

WEDNESDAY — AUGUST 13.

OUR friend Laura was singing cheerfully as she went about her household chores. We had been invited for coffee and were ushered into the sitting-room.

It seemed to be full to overflowing with toys, books and games, but there was no mistaking the genuine welcome in her smile. Her young son was at nursery school, so she had time on her hands to chat. The sound of music came floating from the kitchen as the cups rattled, and I noticed the Lady of the House tapping her foot and humming along.

Later, as we strolled home, she was still singing quietly. "I didn't know you liked country and western music," I teased her.

"This one I shall remember, Francis," she answered. " 'Some days are diamonds, some days are stone' — and this is turning out to be a diamond day."

I smiled in agreement and thought how often simple things can make a day special. We all have it in our power to make a diamond day for someone, if only we take the trouble.

THURSDAY — AUGUST 14.

DO you sometimes get very cross or get into a real flap when things go wrong? Here is a thought on the subject from a former President of the United States, Thomas Jefferson:

"When angry, count 10 before you speak," he used to say. "If very angry, count to 100!"

FRIDAY — AUGUST 15.

OLD sayings passed down to us through the mists of time are just as appropriate today. One of my favourites is: "Be hearty in your salutations; discreet and sincere in your friendships."

SATURDAY — AUGUST 16.

OUR friend Dulcie likes to blow away her cares by reciting to herself these lines from the English poet and writer, Elizabeth Barrett Browning, who died in 1861:

The little cares that fretted me
I lost them yesterday;
Among the fields above the sea
Among the winds at play.

The foolish fears of what may happen
I cast them all away
Among the clover-scented grass
Among the new-mown hay.

Now, doesn't that inspire you to get into the calm and splendour of the great outdoors next time you start to gather too many of the little worries and niggles that hit all of us?

SUNDAY — AUGUST 17.

CHARITY suffereth long, and is kind; charity envieth not; charity vaunteth not itself, is not puffed up.

Corinthians I 13:4

MONDAY — AUGUST 18.

ONE day I felt that the rain had kept me indoors long enough so, donning my waterproof, I set out for a walk. I hadn't gone far when I bumped into Harriet on her way to the post-box.

"It's a bit of a grey day," I observed.

"Grey?" she challenged with a twinkle in her eye. "Why, Francis, it's not like you to be unobservant! Haven't you noticed the different shades of green in that grass? And look at the scarlet berries in the hedgerow, and the many shades of the turning leaves. Even the puddles are reflecting back the silver and violet of the sky. There's colour everywhere, if only you care to look."

So I did look, and I had to concede that she was quite right. Next time I decide it's a grey day, I think I shall try examining my surroundings a little more closely!

TUESDAY — AUGUST 19.

ASK ME

NOT, how did he die, but how did he live?
Not, what did he gain, but what did he give?
These are the units to measure the worth
Of a man as a man, regardless of birth.
Not what was his church, nor what was his creed
But had he befriended those really in need?
Was he ever ready, with a word of good cheer
To bring back a smile, to banish your tear?

Anon.

WEDNESDAY — AUGUST 20.

SITTING in my little summer house, the sunshine-golden day's peace was abruptly shattered by an almighty crash from over the garden wall. There followed a silence which seemed never ending, and then into the silence one small, quavery voice made itself heard:

"Daddy! I love you!"

Whatever young Jamie had broken with his football, I never did find out! But one thing I did realise was that whenever things go wrong, isn't it always the abiding, trusting love of our family which bales us out, dusts us off and sets us back on the right path to face yet another day on life's journey?

THURSDAY — AUGUST 21.

HAVE you ever fallen out with someone and later regretted it? Sometimes it seems like the end of the world and we wonder gloomily if things can ever be the same again.

I always feel encouraged when I think of the words of St Francis de Sales. A 16th-century priest and missionary, he travelled widely to spread the word of God, and saw much of the world and its troubles. Yet still he was able to say:

"A quarrel between friends, when made up, adds a new tie to friendship, as experience shows that the callosity formed round a broken bone makes it stronger than before."

It's a wonderful comparison, and one which we should remember.

PAST AND
PRESENT

FRIDAY — AUGUST 22.

I HAVE just been reading a story about John Logie Baird, the inventor of television. It all happened during the Second World War when bombs were falling relentlessly on London.

John was staying with friends on the outskirts of the city, leaving all his precious work in his laboratory there. He seemed to be very anxious about its safety and, thinking that he needed to rescue a piece of equipment, one of his friends ushered John to his car and drove through the falling bombs to the famous laboratory to put the inventor's mind at rest.

John hurried into the building, emerging a few minutes later with his proud possession under his arm — a little Persian kitten!

SATURDAY — AUGUST 23.

H ERE are more wise words which have stood the test of time:

"It's nice to be important, but it's more important to be nice."

"Be careful of your thoughts, they may become words at any moment."

SUNDAY — AUGUST 24.

B UT now being made free from sin, and become servants to God, ye have your fruit unto holiness, and the end everlasting life.

Romans 6:22

MONDAY — AUGUST 25.
CHANCE ENCOUNTER

*M Y dear old friend, with what delight
Our comradeship has been renewed;
For many a time I've thought of you,
So wistfully, in pensive mood.
In ages gone, my trusted guide,
My mentor, you would take my hand,
To lead me down enchanted roads,
Into many an unknown land.
Then, with the passing years, alas,
Old friends, discarded, dropped away,
Along with all those roseate dreams
That never saw the light of day.
What bliss, then, in that dusty shop,
To find you . . . for in very truth,
You were the joy — beloved book —
And inspiration of my youth!*

Kathleen O'Farrell.

TUESDAY — AUGUST 26.

IT was the day of a Royal wedding and a street party was in full swing. Everyone in the neighbourhood had come, even old Mr Brown who lived on his own and hardly spoke to anyone.

At the end of the meal he stood up and, to everyone's surprise, thanked them all for the lovely birthday treat. Then it dawned on them — he thought it was all for him!

Of course no-one told him and I'm glad to say that he never found out. And after that, they celebrated his birthday every year.

WEDNESDAY — AUGUST 27.

ON the cliffs of Cromer stands a bronze bust in memory of Henry Bloggs, famous coxwain of the Cromer lifeboat. He died in June 1954 after 53 years of service in the local R.N.L.I. which he had joined when only 18 years old.

During his service Henry was instrumental in saving 873 lives and was described as "one of the bravest men who ever lived". But he would have been the first to disclaim such a description, saying that he could not have done it alone. It was teamwork that counted.

He was one of the many brave men who have manned the lifeboats around our coasts since 1824, those who risk their lives on the seas. Sir Winston Churchill once said of a lifeboat:–

"It drives on with a mercy which does not quail in the presence of death; it drives on as a proof, a symbol, a testimony that man is created in the image of God, and that valour and virtue have not perished in the British race."

THURSDAY — AUGUST 28.

COMPLAINERS of this world appear
To sing a mournful song —
"Whenever things are going right,
There must be something wrong."
If only, oh, if only
They would take a great delight
In singing, "When we know what's wrong,
Let's strive to put things right!"

J. M. Robertson.

HOUSE PROUD

FRIDAY — AUGUST 29.

ISN'T it amazing how good can eventually come from the anguish of stressful and traumatic times when it seems that the whole world is against us?

Take, for instance, that famous hymn, "O Love That Wilt Not Let Me Go". It was born on the evening of 6th June 1882 in the manse of Innellan, in Argyll, when Dr George Matheson was feeling at his lowest ebb with the prospect of blindness confronting him.

The world-famous hymn, which was even sung on the slopes of Calvary in 1904 at a Sunday school convention, was always regarded by "Matheson Of Innellan" as his best hymn. Truly, out of the dark night of suffering can often come the most unexpected blessing.

SATURDAY — AUGUST 30.

THE folk the world calls Lucky
Will tell you, every one,
That success comes not by wishing
But from the work they've done.

Don't just wait for things to happen. Start the ball rolling — today. It's up to us to take the initiative.

SUNDAY — AUGUST 31.

AND Jesus came and spake unto them, saying, All power is given unto me in heaven and earth.

Matthew 28:18

September

I'M sure you will be heartened by this tale about Peter, a philosophical friend who had endured a recent tragedy. One afternoon we had a quiet talk, while enjoying the sunshine in his garden, which is his pride and joy.

"Yes, Francis, that was a pretty sticky time in my life, but it is over now and I have put it behind me. I think that one of the things which really helped to keep me going during those dark days was the knowledge that all my friends were willing and anxious to be supportive and helpful."

I nodded. I was remembering the words of Epicurus, the philosopher who lived in Athens in 300 BC: "It's not so much our friends' help that helps us, as the confident knowledge that they will help us."

FAMILY . . . it's one of my favourite words. When I hear it I see a group of adults and children united, not only by blood, but in love, affection and happiness.

And how does it start? Winston Churchill knew. He said: "A family starts with a young man falling in love with a girl. No superior alternative has yet been found."

WEDNESDAY — SEPTEMBER 3.

THE glory of
   The azure sky
The singing of
   The larks on high.

The beauty of
   The sylvan hills
The music of
   The gurgling rills.

The promise of
   The fertile field
The measure of
   The coming yield.

The perfume of
   The new-mown hay
The twilight of
   The dying day.

The shining of
   The Autumn moon
The bounty of
   The harvest soon.

          Glynfab John.

THURSDAY — SEPTEMBER 4.

THINK about these wise words as you go about your various tasks today, particularly if you know you're not really giving something the benefit of your full attention:

"Beware lest your footprints on the sands of time leave only the marks of a heel."

FRIDAY — SEPTEMBER 5.

WE all know them, the people who are never satisfied. No matter what they get, they always seem to be wanting more and more. They are forever striving after something new, never happy with their present circumstances.

The French writer La Rochefoucauld, said, "Before we set our hearts too much on anything, we should examine how happy they are who already possess it."

"I don't want nuthin'," an old Negro woman once said. "I got that a'ready!"

SATURDAY — SEPTEMBER 6.

HAPPINESS SINGS

HAPPINESS sings like a bird flying free
It dances like waves in the silver blue sea,
Happiness laughs like a child having fun
It looks like a bud that unfurls in the sun,
Happiness leaps like a merry March hare
It sparkles like snow in the clear Winter air,
Happiness soars like a rainbow of light
It shines like a star in the black velvet night,
Happiness warms like a smile full of love
And blesses the word like a gift from above.
                                    Margaret Ingall.

SUNDAY — SEPTEMBER 7.

BLESS the Lord, O my soul: and all that is within me, bless his holy name.

                                    Psalms 103:1

THE FRIENDSHIP BOOK

MONDAY — SEPTEMBER 8.

IN 1927 May H. Brahe, an Australian, decided it was time she wrote a new song. Her previous one "I Passed By Your Window" had been very popular. She penned the words "Bless The House", but despite its fine message it did not attract the popularity she expected.

Not until, that is, John McCormack, a well-known singer, decided the song was good, but the title did not add to its attraction. He suggested she should alter it by one word, the replacement of "the" by "this".

His idea of a more personal title succeeded and the song became famous. Sometimes a small change can make a big difference.

TUESDAY — SEPTEMBER 9.

JOHN F. KENNEDY is often remembered as the US President who was assassinated in Dallas. He was loved by many, though like all politicians, was disliked by others. He was, however, a source of inspiration to a great number of people.

I have found several of his speeches encouraging, but these short lines, for me, sum up how we ought to feel about the future: "We should not let our fears hold us back from pursuing our hopes."

How often do we hesitate in a new venture for fear of making a mistake? How many times do we hold back when opportunity comes knocking!

Let us go forward, putting fear behind us and pursuing our hopes wherever they may lead!

THE FRIENDSHIP BOOK

WEDNESDAY — SEPTEMBER 10.

IN his autobiography "Sunset Reflections" author William Riley tells of a Silverdale worthy who owned a pony and trap and took various items down to the railway station each evening.

In this lovely part of Lancashire, which was beloved by Mrs Elizabeth Gaskell, the station is about one and a half miles from the village. On one occasion, the pony trap owner was accompanied by a young passenger. Suddenly, the little boy exclaimed, "All the lights have gone out!"

"Nay, nay, Jack," replied the driver. "It isn't the lights that have gone out. It's because we've come to a dip in the road and can't see 'em. We'll see 'em again soon."

That's a bit like life, isn't it? At times we all encounter disappointments, worry, illness, even the death of a loved one along the way, and feel that all the lights have gone out. Yet, like Jack, we will catch sight of them again in the future when we reach higher ground.

THURSDAY — SEPTEMBER 11.

AT the grand old age of 88, Lord Callaghan, former Prime Minister, handed down some practical advice to men a little younger than himself.

He said, "I tell this to all my friends over 75. Never try to put your socks on standing up."

I hope they heeded him!

<u>FRIDAY — SEPTEMBER 12.</u>

LETTER TO MY CHILDREN

*T*HANK *you for the love you give,*
   And all the joy you've brought,
For all the times when you were small
   And filled each waking thought.
For all the laughter, smiles and tears,
   The studying and stress,
The memory of muddy boots,
   That special party dress!

The days the house filled up with friends
   I never knew each name,
The growing up, the leaving home,
   How quiet life became.
The letters, cards and photographs
   Each play their special part,
But thank you for the love we share,
   Still growing in my heart.

                              Iris Hesselden.

<u>SATURDAY — SEPTEMBER 13.</u>

I VERY much hope that the friends you will be meeting today — and every day of the year — are far removed from those who were once described in this way by the writer Christian Bovee:

"False friends are like our shadow, keeping close to us while we walk in the sunshine, but leaving us the instant we cross into the shade."

The best friends, everywhere, stay with us in both sunshine and shadow.

THE FRIENDSHIP BOOK

TO God only wise, be glory through Jesus Christ for ever. Amen.

Romans 16:27

THE old adage "follow the leader" may sound good advice, but it is often better to strike out on your own and aim at a target of your own making. A wise friend, Edward, who has had much experience of life and living, put this concept to me rather memorably one day.

"Do not follow the path," he said. "Just go right ahead where there is no path — and begin your own trail."

Like the great explorers, there are rewards to be found by "doing your own thing" and being a pioneer.

I WAS interested to hear a radio presenter refer to the music of Schubert as "bottled sunshine". What a lovely thought that we can preserve our own bit of sunshine and keep it for a rainy day!

The possibilities are endless and I'm sure we could each produce our own list of things to create a happy atmosphere. It could be a favourite book or a new hobby, a special corner of the garden or time spent with a good friend.

Whatever you choose, I wish you a day of sunshine.

WEDNESDAY — SEPTEMBER 17.

I RECEIVED an article from a magazine one day, sent by a friend. It was headed "Lessons Learned". These came from people of various ages and I'd like to share a few of them with you today:

"I've learned that if you want to cheer yourself up, you should try cheering someone else up."

(Nathan, aged 14)

"I've learned that you can make someone's day by simply sending them a little note."

(Patricia, aged 34)

"I've learned that no matter what happens, or how bad things seem today, life does go on, and it will be better tomorrow."

(Alexander, aged 48)

"I've learned that life sometimes gives you a second chance."

(Dorothy, aged 62)

"I've learned that it pays to believe in miracles and, to tell the truth, I've seen several."

(Iain, aged 75)

Whatever age we are, we continue to learn, and this is what makes life so exciting.

THURSDAY — SEPTEMBER 18.

HAPPY TOMORROWS

THERE'S hope to be found in the future,
Each day brings along a new start,
With the promise of happy tomorrows —
If you lift up and open your heart.

Sarah Ashcroft.

FRIDAY — SEPTEMBER 19.

A YOUNG Chinese boy living in Manila in the Philippine Islands once wanted a bicycle. He saved the equivalent of three pounds, and then decided that he wanted something else even more — to help his own people, who were starving and suffering terribly under oppression.

He went to the bakery and spent all his savings on sacks of bread. These he took to the offices of the China Relief Committee. Now that posed a problem — they didn't want to tell him that the bread would be mouldy before it got to the needy people in China. But someone suggested selling it as "Patriotic Bread" to Chinese people in Manila.

It sold readily and the boy's three pounds soon became ten. Sales of further batches of bread increased until three hundred pounds were raised. This was sent to China in the boy's name.

An American in Manila heard the story, as later did Mrs Henry Ford, who sent a cheque to buy the boy a bike. He still wanted to help, so decided to hire out his bike, and send the money raised to the relief fund. Still the story goes on — bikes for hire became the main support of a Christian home in China for orphan boys.

A miracle indeed but for any miracle to happen action must follow words.

SATURDAY — SEPTEMBER 20.

IF you find an acorn or a hazelnut on a path, plant it in good soil for it to grow. You could be giving your grandchildren a wood to play in.

THE FRIENDSHIP BOOK

<u>SUNDAY — SEPTEMBER 21.</u>

THY dead men shall live, together with my dead body shall they arise. Awake and sing, ye that dwell in dust; for thy dew is as the dew of herbs, and the earth shall cast out the dead.

Isaiah 26:19

<u>MONDAY — SEPTEMBER 22.</u>

ALFRED Wainwright is famous for his Lakeland Guides with their great wealth of detail about the area, but he loved nature in all forms and in all places. He once wrote:

"There is beauty everywhere . . . You do not need money in your pocket to walk through a field of wild flowers. We have more blessings than we could ever count."

Sometimes, if we are a little down in the mouth, let us take another look around us and remember his words: "There is beauty everywhere", then perhaps we can count just a few of our many blessings.

<u>TUESDAY — SEPTEMBER 23.</u>

THE Lady of the House and I laughed when John, a neighbour, told us how his hearing aid occasionally emits a high-pitched squeal that can be heard by anyone near him. His granddaughter was sitting on his lap one day when the device started to beep.

Surprised, little Lorraine looked up at him and said, "Oh, Grandpa, you've got e-mail!"

WEDNESDAY — SEPTEMBER 24.

WHAT would we do without our climate? Even with a complete stranger we can immediately start a conversation by talking about the weather. It is a subject guaranteed to break down all barriers yet, in a different sense, climate can also be a barrier for so much depends on an individual.

Take the person who is chilly to everyone they meet — they pass that chilliness on. Then there's the person who's cloudy, full of gloom, leaving you feeling miserable. And what about the person who knows how to put the whole world to rights, thundering on about everyone and everything? Well, at least that climate is invigorating, if somewhat exhausting!

Then there's the person with a sunny climate, beaming at you in greeting, creating an immediate warm feeling. It makes you feel that even if the sun isn't actually shining, it will be very soon.

It reminds me of a "climate" chorus sung at Sunday school years ago:

Jesus wants me for a sunbeam,
A sunbeam, a sunbeam,
Jesus wants me for a sunbeam,
And I'll be a sunbeam for Him.

THURSDAY — SEPTEMBER 25.

HERE are some simple words for us to think about as we welcome another morning:

"Each day comes bearing its own gifts — be sure to untie the ribbons."

FRIDAY — SEPTEMBER 26.

A SCHOOL swimming gala was under way, and one of the competitors was a young Scout who was somewhat put out to be told that because of some infringement of the rules he was being disqualified. The boy remonstrated with the judges but to no avail.

Then he played his trump card. Rising to his full five feet he vowed that the matter would be referred to "the very highest authority in the land — my Mum!" And there could be no better mediator!

SATURDAY — SEPTEMBER 27.

A SYMPATHETIC friendly face
When we are feeling down,
A cheery smile that warms the heart
And smoothes away the frown.
The unexpected gesture,
A soft and gentle touch,
The tender tone of well-meant words
Are things that mean so much.

Kindliness that can't be bought,
Concern that is sincere,
The understanding of a friend
With ready listening ear.
These are only little things
And yet they play a part,
Refreshment for the spirit
And healing for the heart.

Kathleen Gillum.

SUNDAY — SEPTEMBER 28.

FOR ye were as sheep going astray; but are now returned unto the Shepherd and Bishop of your souls.

Peter I 2:25

MONDAY — SEPTEMBER 29.

IN a strange kind of way life reminds me of a strong football team, one which we can all support to create a winning combination. With that thought in mind, the eleven "players" worthy of consideration in that context are as follows:

Enthusiam
Hope   Courage   Will-power   Toleration
Friendship   Understanding   Compassion
Sincerity   Endeavour   Perseverance

Under the name Universal United, such a team must surely score positive success!

TUESDAY — SEPTEMBER 30.

I NEVER cease to admire the enthusiasm with which so many people go climbing the world's hills and mountains. The writer John Muir had this to say:

"Climb the mountains and get their good tidings: Nature's peace will flow into you as sunshine into flowers. The winds will blow their freshness into you, and the storms their energy. Soon you will find that your cares are dropping off like Autumn leaves."

October

SINCE 1991, 1st October has been designated by the United Nations as The International Day Of Older Persons. In recognition of this, Pope John Paul II wrote a letter to the elderly throughout the world calling on them to rejoice in their age and experience saying, "There is an urgent need to recover a correct perspective on life as a whole."

He ended with these words of encouragement: "Live with serenity the years that the Lord has granted you."

I was reminded of the lovely words of this hymn:

Lord, for the years your love has kept and guided,
Urged and inspired us, cheered us on our way,
Sought us and saved us, pardoned and provided:
Lord of the years, we bring our thanks today.

IN southern Germany and Austria people don't say "Hello" or "Good morning" in the same way that we do. Instead they smile and say "Greet God!" It's a lovely way of giving thanks for the gift of a new day and of celebrating it with all those around us.

FRIDAY — OCTOBER 3.

IAN GREGORY, journalist turned United Reform Church minister, was getting more than a bit fed up with the amount of rudeness and bad language that he seemed to be experiencing.

So in 1986 he initiated The Polite Society, with a code of courteous conduct which included a daily resolution to "deal with every situation as I meet it with the utmost consideration for other people's feelings." Ten years later, The Polite Society became the Campaign For Courtesy, aiming to encourage those who value good manners. The first Friday in October is now designated as a National Day Of Courtesy.

There is a belief that "even a small advance in courtesy would make this country cheaper to run, more productive, healthier, happier, and less at the mercy of anti-social elements."

Courtesy and good manners still leave a positive impression — don't they?

SATURDAY — OCTOBER 4.

JOY cometh in the morning
As with the break of day,
Dark ghosts of pain and sorrow
Slip silently away.

Then as dawn's finger beckons,
Small birds begin to sing,
And over all, in blessing
Hope spreads her shining wings.
                    C. M. Douglas.

SUNDAY — OCTOBER 5.

BLESSED are they that do his commandments, that they may have right to the tree of life, and may enter in through the gates into the city.

Revelation 22:14

MONDAY — OCTOBER 6.

IN her Journal, Helen Keller describes her rediscovery of a portrait in relief of Sir Arthur Pearson, who had lost his sight just before the Great War.

He refused to give in, and was a prime mover in the development of the (now Royal) National Institute For The Blind and the founding of St Dunstan's hostel for soldiers, sailors (and later airmen) blinded in the service of their country.

In conversation with Miss Keller, he revealed that he had created St Dunstan's so that blinded folk released from hospital "might come into a little world where things they could not do would be forgotten, and the principal concern would be with things they could do."

Sir Arthur Pearson also offered to have the books Helen Keller wished to read embossed into braille at no cost. Such was the man, founder of "The Daily Express", "the blind spirit of Fleet Street".

TUESDAY — OCTOBER 7.

SUCCESS in marriage is more than finding the right person; it is a matter of being the right person.   Rabbi B. R. Brickner.

WEDNESDAY — OCTOBER 8.

A READER called Jemima told me the following story which I'd like to share with you. Once, when having afternoon tea with friends, she withdrew a handkerchief from her pocket and a piece of tinsel fell on to the table. Now, while we are all used to being knee-deep in silver and gold tinsel in the festive season, it's an entirely different matter during the glorious days of Autumn. So what had happened?

It seems that Jemima's minister, the Rev David McKay of St Columba's Parish Church in Largs, had urged the children in his Sunday school to present every member of the congregation with a tiny piece of tinsel during the bleak days of January. The idea was that it should be kept throughout the year, to remind everyone that kindness, goodwill and genuine friendship should never have a "sell-by" date.

THURSDAY — OCTOBER 9.

WE tend to forget what great advances there have been in recent times in so many areas of life. Even so, it came as a surprise to me when I learned that early church hassocks simply consisted of tufts or clumps of matted vegetation cut from boggy ground and then trimmed and shaped for the comfort and convenience of worshippers.

With today's added comfort of velvet embroidered hassocks, perhaps this is as good a time as any to kneel in prayer?

THE FRIENDSHIP BOOK

FRIDAY — OCTOBER 10.

A TEACHER friend, during an absence from school due to illness, was greatly cheered to get a number of home-made get-well cards from her pupils.

One six-year-old boy had drawn a delightful picture of his absent teacher, depicting her leaping with glorious abandon over a crescent moon. Although the drawing itself was self-explanatory, the caption was the icing on the cake:

Dear Miss Macdonald,
I hope you'll soon be feeling as fit as a fidel.
Love from Tommy.

SATURDAY — OCTOBER 11.

I RECEIVED a letter one morning from our friend Penny, who lives in Tasmania. She was writing about our mutual reaction to some dramatic happenings in the world, and then she added these words which reflected her appreciation of nature Down Under:

"I have just lifted my head to look out at the garden, and I see the beauty of the Autumn leaves, the reds, the greens, and the orange and browns. The world is an amazing place.

"It's a beautiful day, fluffy clouds floating across a pale blue sky, a slight nip of frost in the air. And, yes, there is a kookaburra calling in the distance."

I hope you agree that, every now and then, it is good to lift our heads from work and our daily worries, and take time to look at the wonderful world that is all around us.

GOLDEN GLADE

SUNDAY — OCTOBER 12.

AND early in the morning he came again into the temple, and all the people came unto him: and he sat down, and taught them.

John 8:2

MONDAY — OCTOBER 13.

"YOU see that one — it's mine!" Old Millie was pointing at a brick in our new church extension. One of the ways the money was raised to build it was by inviting members of the congregation to pay for a brick. Millie did so and has convinced herself that a certain brick in the wall is hers.

"Take away that brick and the wall would fall down," she says. "I'm helping to keep our church standing."

Indeed she is.

TUESDAY — OCTOBER 14.

LAST century there was a famous chess player, Richard Reti, who declared that in chess the player who finds himself in an inferior position, possibly with an apparently lost game is, tactically speaking, holding an advantage for his case leaves room for most improvement.

A good lesson for life in general, surely. John Bunyan wrote: "He that is down needs fear no fall."

In other words, when you hit rock-bottom the only way to go is up. So when we feel down, let's start climbing!

WEDNESDAY — OCTOBER 15.

MOVING FORWARD

WE must keep moving forward,
No time for standing still,
The past and present urge us on
Towards that distant hill.
Towards that bright horizon
Where hopes and dreams come true,
Where joy and peace and happiness
All wait for me and you.

The past had much to offer,
And lessons we should learn,
But yesterday has slipped away
And never will return.
Tomorrow holds a promise,
Today's for you and me,
So keep on moving forward,
The best is yet to be!

Iris Hesselden.

THURSDAY — OCTOBER 16.

CRITICISM can be helpful but only when it is fair and kindly meant. Abraham Lincoln said we all have the right to criticise — if we also have the heart to help.

I like, too, the comment by Archbishop Garbett: "Any fool can criticise, and too many of them do."

Someone else remarked that the only sure way to avoid the critics would be to do nothing, say nothing, and be nothing.

THE FRIENDSHIP BOOK

FRIDAY — OCTOBER 17.

PERHAPS today is special for you or a member of your family? Or for a friend or neighbour? I am thinking, in particular, of a heartwarming event that happens for so many families everywhere — the birth of a baby.

It's not just the happy mother and proud father who share this memorable moment of joy. The older generation in the family also have reason to celebrate, as an unknown writer once put it:

"When a child is born, two precious gifts are received . . . a grandchild and a grandparent."

SATURDAY — OCTOBER 18.

HAVE you ever climbed a steep hill? The worst of it is that as you toil and labour from rock to rock you keep believing the summit is just in front of you. Then you realise that yet another bit of the hill was hidden and there still remains another section.

Sometimes you feel so frustrated and so tired that you think it's not worth going on, and you might as well turn and go back. However, it's only once you reach the summit at last that you see what you have achieved, and you can look behind and feel that the struggle was not in vain after all.

SUNDAY — OCTOBER 19.

BE not forgetful to entertain strangers: for thereby some have entertained angels unawares.

Hebrews 13: 2

MONDAY — OCTOBER 20.

AUTUMN is a favourite time of the year, even if it does herald the approach of Winter and shorter, colder days. I love the shades of brown, red and yellow which leaves turn, giving the trees a majestic beauty.

The Lady of the House and I were taking an Autumn walk through the village one rather chilly day when we met an old acquaintance of ours. Edward is a keen gardener and nature lover. Exchanging a word or two about the change of season which was obviously making itself felt, I commented, "It is rather sad when the leaves fall and trees are left bare and lose much of their beauty."

"Don't look at it that way!" he replied. "You can still admire their splendid shapes and form." Edward is quite a philosopher and added, "You know, Francis, doesn't it remind you of ourselves? When we are stripped of our decorations and fine clothes, we are revealed as we really are."

How true. We enjoyed the remaining walk, observing how graceful and interesting the shapes of the trees were.

TUESDAY — OCTOBER 21.

THE American columnist Anne Landers once offered this thought-provoking piece of advice to her readers:

"The true measure of a man is how he treats someone who can do him absolutely no good."

Now, isn't that as fine a yardstick as any?

WEDNESDAY — OCTOBER 22.

WE are often told that these days a lot of people only care about money. But on the odd occasion when I'm tempted to accept that gloomy verdict, I'm always able to comfort myself by recalling these replies given to that age-old question — in the event of a fire, what is the first thing you would try to rescue from your house?

The fact that so many people will immediately say that photographs, letters and mementoes are their choice, rather than more expensive possessions, always reassures me. I'm sure it confirms our real values in life; we instinctively recognise that links with family and friends are worth far more than the most expensive goods.

THURSDAY — OCTOBER 23.

WHAT do we do with the moments we save
As we rush through the course of the day?
If we dash to the post, or run for a bus,
Cut corners along all the way.

Will the minutes we save add up to an hour
To be used later on? No, alas,
Moments are fleeting, and time doesn't wait
But goes on, and life's days and years pass.

Time is God-given. The best we can do
Is to come to Him every new day,
And ask him to fill every moment in time
With his peace, as we go on our way.
Anon.

FRIDAY — OCTOBER 24.

SARAH is no longer young and is also almost housebound, but when the Lady of the House and I popped round to wish her a happy birthday, we were impressed by the number of cards already on display.

Seeing my surprise, she smiled. "Penfriends, Francis, that's the secret! You see, I was an only child, and had a very few relatives, so right from my schooldays I made up my mind to forge friendship links, and never allow the bond to break through distance or neglect.

"And I've certainly reaped the reward," she added, "for almost every week brings me news and greetings from one part of the world or another. I may not be able to get out very much, but I never feel alone or forgotten."

Isn't it nice to see how tending the seeds of friendship can bring forth such a harvest of happiness!

SATURDAY — OCTOBER 25.

"NEVER be afraid of landing in life's bunkers if you've tried your best shot."

So, go on, try — there can be no finer aim in life!

SUNDAY — OCTOBER 26.

FOR God hath not given us the spirit of fear; but of power, and of love, and of a sound mind.

Timothy II 1:7

THE FRIENDSHIP BOOK

I HAVE been reading a favourite book, Fraser Darling's "Island Farm". As a biologist, he and his wife Bobbie settled in the 1940s on a remote island off the coast of Scotland.

They had a rugged outdoor lifestyle and one of their tasks was to rebuild the quay to make a harbour for their boat. It was a back-breaking job and one that took the skin from their fingertips.

"But," wrote Darling, "peace came in through the fingertips from that touch of the stone as we fitted it to its appointed place and found it good and firm. There is great peace to be got from hands in use; the control of tools was a co-ordination which reached the whole man in us."

It is something that many have found to be true — in a time of difficulty, become absorbed in something that involves your mind and your hands. This can bring immense satisfaction.

OUR friend Joan keeps her favourite thoughts and sentiments pasted neatly into a little notebook that is already over half full. I once asked her if she has any particular favourite among the dozens she has collected. Here is the one she chose:

"A hundred years from now it will not matter what my bank account was, the sort of house I lived in, or the kind of car I drove . . . but the world may be just that much different because I was important in the life of a little child."

WEDNESDAY — OCTOBER 29.

SOME of my brightest friends are the oldest in years, but youthful in how they look at life. One 93-year-old American friend keeps telling me: "Never forget the kid in you — that's where you started!" I would also like to share with you today these two thoughts on feeling younger than you are:

"Youth is happy because it has the ability to see beauty. Anyone who keeps the ability to see beauty never grows old."

Franz Kafka.

"Youth is not a time of life; it is a state of mind; it is not a matter of rosy cheeks, red lips and supple knees; it is a matter of the will, quality of the imagination, a vigour of the emotions; it is the freshness of the deep springs of life."

Samuel Ullman.

THURSDAY — OCTOBER 30.

"REGARDLESS of how much money you have," said a writer in a magazine, "wisdom has to be bought on the instalment plan."

Like so many of the good things in life, you acquire it in stages, slowly and steadily until, finally, you can exercise it in all its strength.

FRIDAY — OCTOBER 31.

"HAVE a heart that never hardens, and a temper that never tires, and a touch that never hurts."

Charles Dickens.

November

SATURDAY — NOVEMBER 1.

THE Lady of the House and I are fond of our little book-room. It is perhaps not quite grand enough to be styled a library, but we think it's a very pleasant and relaxing place in which to sit and read.

One evening we lit and enjoyed, in quiet companionship, our first log fire of the year of sweet-smelling fruitwood. It was then, when turning the pages of my scrapbook, that I came across these words: "Shall we make a new rule of life from tonight always to try to be a little kinder than is necessary?"

What a good idea, for kind words and deeds always bring sunshine in their wake.

These words were written by the man who wrote that well-loved play, "Peter Pan", a tale for all ages — the novelist and playwright Sir James Barrie who was born in 1860 in Kirriemuir.

SUNDAY — NOVEMBER 2.

AND keep the charge of the Lord thy God, to walk in his ways, to keep his statutes, and his commandments, and his judgments, and his testimonies, as it is written in the law of Moses.

Kings 1 2:3

MONDAY — NOVEMBER 3.

THE HEDGEHOG

UNDERNEATH the hawthorn bush
  Amid the grass and thistles,
There crouched a little hedgehog,
  A brooding mass of bristles.

As he lay unmoving,
  Impervious to my touch,
I thought, even humans oft-times
  Scarce differ from him much.

We develop bristly armour
  And curl up in a ball,
Loth to leave a comfy nest
  To answer neighbour's call.

So let's leave to the hedgehog
  Those stubborn, spiky features,
E'er keen to lend a helping-hand
  To all our fellow-creatures.

                    Joe H. McGibbon.

TUESDAY — NOVEMBER 4.

A KEEN angler friend tells me that he once
caught sight of a notice beside an Irish river
which contained the following three words: "Fly
Fishing Only".

Underneath some prankster had not been able
to resist adding, tongue firmly in cheek, this
observation: "Only three bluebottles from each
day's catch!"

THE FRIENDSHIP BOOK

<u>WEDNESDAY — NOVEMBER 5.</u>

YOUNG Joanne has just returned home from a year in Nepal, where she was teaching in a remote country school.

"It was a wonderful experience," she said, "although I did feel a little homesick from time to time. But one of the things that really helped was the present Mum gave me.

"You see, as a surprise, she'd bought an audio cassette tape for me, and compiled a wide-ranging selection of all sorts of things — snatches of my favourite music, the sounds of birdsong recorded in our garden, and words of good wishes and encouragement from all our friends and neighbours.

"If ever I felt lonely, all I needed to do was switch on and I'd know that even though I was many miles from home, in some ways it was no distance at all."

What a wonderfully tangible reminder that however far from our loved ones we may be, it's never too far for loving thoughts to reach us.

<u>THURSDAY — NOVEMBER 6.</u>

OUR friend Pat is never short of good friends who will whisper that welcome word of encouragement when things go a little wrong. She says, "I believe that friends are quiet angels who lift us to our feet when our wings have trouble remembering how to fly."

Words that create an almost perfect image, well worth keeping in mind.

THE WAY
AHEAD

FRIDAY — NOVEMBER 7.

AGE Concern, with the help of volunteers, set up an excellent "Keeping In Touch" phone link. The loneliness or anxiety of many is helped by a friendly phone call from a volunteer. Many of the volunteers of all ages say how much they, too, enjoy their regular chats.

This is especially so for the caller who rings Don, a retired builder. He has a great sense of humour, and takes pride in having a joke ready to relate. Here's an example:

"Have you heard about the farmer whose 'Private' and 'Trespassers Will Be Prosecuted' notices had been constantly ignored, so he put up the following sign by the gate to his grazing fields: The farmer permits you to cross his field for free, but the bull will charge."

Thank goodness for people like Don with a sense of humour and, above all, their willingness to share lighter moments with others.

SATURDAY — NOVEMBER 8.

ARE you good at saying "I'm sorry"? Whether you are or not, I'd like you to share today these words on a poster in a busy social club:

"An apology is a good way to have the last word!"

SUNDAY — NOVEMBER 9.

GREET them that love us in the faith. Grace be with you all. Amen.

Titus 3:15

THE FRIENDSHIP BOOK

MONDAY — NOVEMBER 10.

VISITING the Holy Land, a visitor was entranced by the sound of what appeared to be a shepherd's pipe sounding a plaintive melody. It turned out to be played by a young Arab who was leading a small donkey. When the visitor took a close look at his flute, he found himself looking at half a gun barrel.

The Arab had found a rifle left behind on the hillside. He'd filed it in half, made holes in it, turning an instrument of war into an instrument of peace.

While in Japan, a visiting missionary noticed a little cross which had been given to the pastor by Christians from Korea, many of whom had unhappy memories of the period when their native land was occupied by Japanese soldiers. What was different about that little cross? It had been fashioned out of used brass bullet cartridges, and now stood as a sign of peace and reconciliation.

Two encouraging examples of weapons of war being turned into instruments of peace, reconciliation and friendship.

TUESDAY — NOVEMBER 11.

NOT long ago I came across these happy and cheerful words from the pen of the American writer, Julia Dorr, and I thought they would make a good thought for today:

The year grows rich as it groweth old,
And life's latest sands are its sands of gold!

WEDNESDAY — NOVEMBER 12.

WHAT is greatness? The first answer I would give is that it is not found only in the famous. The novelist Charles Reade said, "Not a day passes over the earth, but men and women of no note do great deeds."

Someone else remarked: "The greatest truths are the simplest, and so are the greatest men."

Best of all I love this from the Scots politician Bonar Law: "If I am a great man, then a good many of the great men of history are frauds!"

THURSDAY — NOVEMBER 13.

I RECEIVED this little story from a reader in New Zealand and I thought that you might like to share it today.

A group of friends were sitting around a table lightheartedly discussing what questions they would ask God when they got to the Pearly Gates. Not surprisingly, there were a lot of different questions but one friend who usually joined in group discussions with gusto was very quiet. After a time the others sitting round the table looked at her and said, "June — well, what would you ask God?"

Her reply came quietly: "Can I please come in?"

A loud silence descended upon the table . . .

FRIDAY — NOVEMBER 14.

THERE is an old Spanish saying which says so much in a few words:

"When a friend asks, there is no tomorrow."

SATURDAY — NOVEMBER 15.

HAVE you ever heard of the smile chain? Someone might be feeling particularly glum, but then a friend, or perhaps a complete stranger, does something to brighten up their day. Then they do the same for others, often without realising it.

Louise was feeling dispirited at the thought of taking on extra work responsibilities. This entailed e-mail during a colleague's absence.

On her first morning, she discovered that a friend had sent her an amusing animated electronic postcard which depicted a well-known cartoon character grappling with the intricacies of a computer. The preoccupied expression, the keyboarding mistakes . . . all rang a bell. Then came the animated image's pièce de résistance — and she laughed aloud. So, too, did her colleagues.

When Louise passed on the amusing cartoon to a friend overseas who had been through a somewhat traumatic time, she received this e-mail reply:

Did anyone ever tell you
How good you've made others feel?
Now I know somebody out there is smiling,
Sending a love that is so real.
So go on, send out a smile today!

SUNDAY — NOVEMBER 16.

TRUST in the Lord with all thine heart; and lean not to thine own understanding.

Proverbs 3: 5

THE FRIENDSHIP BOOK

MONDAY — NOVEMBER 17.

THEY say that life's a highway,
*   A journey through the years,*
With milestones made of memories
*   And sometimes washed with tears.*
And now and then, a toll gate
*   Demands a higher price,*
But look ahead, a better view
*   Will beckon and entice.*

A rough road and a steep road
*   This highway we must take,*
With many signposts on the way.
*   Decisions we must make.*
But as we travel onward
*   There's beauty all the while,*
And love to spread a golden glow
*   And brighten every mile.*

Iris Hesselden.

TUESDAY — NOVEMBER 18.

"FRANCIS, I was frightened the whole time."
Believe it or not, the man who told me that was a war hero and he was talking about an incredible act of bravery for which he received a medal. So, do I think any less of him because I know he was afraid?

Of course not. The truth is I admire him all the more. Somehow he conquered his fears and did what had to be done.

When I think of him, I remember the saying that courage is not absence of fear, but the mastering of it.

WEDNESDAY — NOVEMBER 19.

ONE afternoon I met Maureen as she came out of the optician's clutching a brand-new pair of spectacles.

"I feel quite ashamed of myself, Francis," she admitted. "For months now I've been putting off getting reading glasses, simply because I didn't want to admit that I needed them. And then I realised just how silly I was being.

"Here I am, lucky enough to live in an age where not only are spectacles readily available, but there are also plenty of wonderful books to read, and electric light to see them by. It would be ridiculous to reject so many blessings just out of vanity." She smiled sheepishly. "I think my new glasses are already beginning to help me see a lot of things more clearly!"

Well said, Maureen. We should all try to open our eyes to the joys of everyday miracles.

THURSDAY — NOVEMBER 20.

WHAT TO DO

WHEN things go wrong, as well they might,
  The thing to do to put them right
Is try the very best you can
  To activate a helpful plan,
That can create a little hope
  And thereby formulate some scope
In cultivating quite a strong
  Defence whenever things go wrong.

                    J. M. Robertson.

FRIDAY — NOVEMBER 21.

HANDS are a necessity, not just for obvious things like writing but also for helping friends and neighbours. Max Bygraves, the entertainer, had a big hit with his popular singalong number "You Need Hands", spelling out the many jobs and functions they do.

On this subject I'm reminded of a bit of advice my grandmother passed on to me. "Remember, Francis," she said, "if you ever need a helping hand, you will find one at the end of your arm."

Then she would add, "You'll also discover, as you go through life, just why you have two hands. One is for helping yourself, the other for helping others."

SATURDAY — NOVEMBER 22.

FEED your birds, especially in Winter, whether you live in the centre of the busiest town or right in the heart of the country. There is no joy like that of seeing a robin flying down to the crumbs, his little chest puffed out and his bright eyes dancing.

Never throw away a crust in Winter — remember that it could be lunch for a hungry sparrow.

SUNDAY — NOVEMBER 23.

THEREFORE being justified by faith, we have peace with God through our Lord Jesus Christ.

Romans 5:1

MONDAY — NOVEMBER 24.

ON a sightseeing walk through an attractive village, our friend Doris was somewhat disconcerted to have her friendly "Hello!" to a woman in her front garden greeted by stony silence. What a rude woman, Doris thought, about to walk on.

But something made her stop, and she cupped her hand round a beautiful rose blossom, one of many which were tumbling over the fence.

"I see Peace is responding to your care this year," Doris smiled.

The transformation was immediate — the woman's frown disappeared, her eyes lit up joyfully and eagerly she began to relate how she'd nurtured the rose bush through long, cold Winter days, pruned it, and fed it the correct rose fertiliser . . . A story of great love and care.

Discover a person's special interest, find something sincere to say, be appreciative and, in no time, bridges will be built.

TUESDAY — NOVEMBER 25.

SIR Walter Scott certainly knew the value of words, as is shown in this short quotation in which every single word counts:

"Look back, and smile at perils past."

It says it all, doesn't it, especially regarding the negative aspect of pointless worrying, and that is something we've all done over "perils past". Don't you agree?

EITHER
WAY UP

THE FRIENDSHIP BOOK

A CHURCH I know has a very nice custom of acknowledging birthdays. Each Sunday the congregation is asked if anyone has a birthday in the coming week and, when hands are raised, people are given a card with the church's greeting.

Then everyone sings a special version of "Happy Birthday To You" and gets a round of applause. It brings together the youngest and oldest in the church family.

The original happy birthday song was published as long ago as 1893 by two American sisters, Mildred J. Hill and Dr Patty Smith Hill, and it is among the best-known songs in the English language. It has been sung at private parties, junior school assemblies and by the crowds outside Buckingham Palace when the Queen Mother celebrated her 100th birthday.

If today happens to be your special day may I say: "Happy birthday to you!"

FLOWERS OF FRIENDSHIP

SUCH tiny seeds the flowers bear,
And borne upon the winds of chance
May find a lodging here and there
In which to rest — a happenstance.

But seeds they are and so remain
Thus dormant 'til receptive hearts,
With warmth, the cycle once again
Of growth and flowering slowly starts.

Earle Douglas.

FRIDAY — NOVEMBER 28.

WHAT a great deal we can learn from the animal and bird world about the ways they treat members of their own group.

I have been reading some interesting facts about geese. By flying in V-shaped formations each bird flies in the slipstream of the bird in front, so the whole flock can increase its flying range by 71 per cent over a single bird flying alone. Also, while flying in formation, the geese at the back honk at those in front to give encouragement. Should one of the geese be sick or wounded, then two of the flock drop out and follow to help the injured one.

If we follow the example of the geese, we can offer our support to those in need. In the words of Charles Wesley:

Help us to help each other, Lord,
Each other's cross to bear,
Let each his friendly aid afford,
And feel his brother's care.

SATURDAY — NOVEMBER 29.

IT is nearly St Andrew's Day, and I have chosen a typically Scottish thought for you today:

A man o' words, and no' o' deeds,
is like a garden fu' o' weeds.

Don't you agree that a bit of action speaks louder than words?

SUNDAY — NOVEMBER 30.

AND the disciples were filled with joy, and with the Holy Ghost.

Acts 13:52

December

FRIENDSHIP'S TOUCH

*W*HEN I need a helping hand,
You're always there to understand,
To offer with your welcome smile,
Your friendship, which is so worthwhile.
A little kindness means so much,
And shows the warmth of friendship's touch,
Relied upon in times of need,
To really mean a friend indeed!

Elizabeth Gozney.

DO you have a difficult task ahead today? The tendency for many of us is to procrastinate. One day, I was given a useful tip by John, a friend who used to put off most jobs. He told me how he'd discovered that tackling what seems formidable brings much satisfaction, even pleasure.

Epicurus, the fourth-century Greek philosopher, discovered this when he wrote; "The greater the difficulty, the more the glory is in surmounting it."

Good food for thought here, surely!

THE FRIENDSHIP BOOK

SALLY, a friend much respected for good judgment and an ability to hand out sensible advice, was once telling her cousin to be less demanding. She took the young man aside, and asked him to sit down quietly.

I have always remembered the words that Sally used that day. "We are here," she said, "to add what we can to life — not to get what we can from it."

A tip, for this or any other day, that is well worth remembering.

WHAT a lovely thing it is
To have a loyal friend,
Someone who understands us
And on whom we can depend.
A friend who sees and knows our faults
And likes us anyway,
And never seems to take offence
At anything we say.

One who helps us in our troubles
Stands by us in our need —
Such friendship transcends barriers
Of colour, race or creed.
For friendship is a precious gift
And we should always treasure
The ones who share our grief, our joy,
Our heartache and our pleasure.

Kathleen Gillum.

FRIDAY — DECEMBER 5.

HOW often we say, "If only there were more hours in a day," or "If only I had the time." Looking through some old family papers, I came across these wise words which I'd like to pass on to you:

Take time to think, it is the source of power.
Take time to play, it is the secret of
*   perpetual youth.*
Take time to read, it is the fountain of wisdom.
Take time to pray, it is the greatest power
*   on earth.*
Take time to be friendly, it is the road to
*   happiness.*
Take time to love and be loved, it is a
*   God-given privilege.*
Take time to laugh, it is the music of the soul.
Take time to give, days are too short to be selfish.
Take time to work, it is the price of success.
Take time to be charitable, it is the greatest of
*   the virtues.*
Take time to be good to others, it is the key
*   to heaven.*

SATURDAY — DECEMBER 6.

HERE'S a wise thought for you to consider today. It was seen on a notice at the foot of a clock tower:

"One thing you can learn by watching this clock is that it passes time by keeping both of its hands busy."

SUNDAY — DECEMBER 7.

WHEN Christ, who is our life, shall appear, then shall ye also appear with him in glory.

Colossians 3:4

MONDAY — DECEMBER 8.

FIRE is frightening. I once watched a television programme about forest fires in Australia, where thousands of square miles of countryside can be devastated, wildlife perishes and fields of barren charcoal are all that is left behind.

Several months later the same area was filmed again. Among the blackened plants green shoots were appearing — the bush was already re-establishing itself. It seems that some species actually need fire before they can release seed. Nature is truly amazing.

The Aborigines found this out centuries ago and burned down forests to renew them. Did they find this out by accident? Perhaps — and yet it was as if a Divine Hand had guided their fore-fathers many centuries before.

TUESDAY — DECEMBER 9.

TWO thoughts to keep in mind today — and any day, for that matter:

There's only one thing better than a friend you can trust; and that's a friend who trusts you.

Use whatever talents you possess. The woods would be very silent if no birds sang except those that sang the best.

CHRISTMAS
CHEER

THE FRIENDSHIP BOOK

<u>WEDNESDAY — DECEMBER 10.</u>

YOUNG Andrew had gone to stay with his grandmother and she had given him an old family Bible to look at. He was fascinated by the pictures and when a leaf which had been pressed among the pages fell out, he squealed:

"Look what I've found, Gran!"

"What is it?" she asked.

With astonishment in his voice he replied, "I think it's Adam's clothes!"

<u>THURSDAY — DECEMBER 11.</u>

OUR old friend Mary came across these lines one day as she was about to make a start to her long list of Christmas cards to be written, stamped and posted:

I have a list of folk I know, all written in a book,
And every year at Christmas time I go and take
a look.
And that is when I realise that these names are
a part,
Not of the book they're written in, but of my
very heart.

Every year when Christmas comes I realise anew,
The biggest gift life can give is knowing folk
like you.
May the Spirit of Christmas that forever
endures,
Leave its rich blessings in the hearts of you
and yours.

FRIDAY — DECEMBER 12.

DO you carry forward, into tomorrow, some of the problems and niggles which may have affected you today and still seem to be hanging about? Well, here's what R. W. Emerson had to say on the matter:

"Finish each day and be done with it. You have done what you could. Some blunders and absurdities no doubt crept in; forget them as soon as you can. Tomorrow is a new day; begin it well and serenely and with too high a spirit to be encumbered with your old nonsense."

In other words, start your new day with the slate wiped clean.

SATURDAY — DECEMBER 13.

JOHANN Wolfgang von Goethe, the German philosopher, once said: "Correction does much, but encouragement does so much more."

I'm also reminded of what the writer Elizabeth Harrison advised: "Those who lift the world upward and onward are those who encourage more than criticise."

Let's stop looking for things to criticise. Isn't it better to look, instead, at how we can encourage our friends and neighbours? Try it today!

SUNDAY — DECEMBER 14.

AND ye my flock, the flock of my pasture, are men, and I am your God, saith the Lord God.

Ezekiel 34:31

THE FRIENDSHIP BOOK

A LITTLE boy asked his Sunday School teacher, "Please, Miss, does God have a mobile phone?"

Not an easy question to answer, but tactfully she told him, "I suppose He must have, for in his own way, He keeps in touch with lots of people every day."

"Mmm," mused the young lad. "Does he not get a row for using it too much? My sister does!"

E ACH December since 1989 Austrian Scouts and Guides have helped to pass on the Peace Light from Bethlehem. The light is permanently situated in the Grotto in Bethlehem where the birth of Jesus Christ is celebrated.

An Austrian child lights a lamp from the flame and takes it to Austria where it travels all over the country, thanks to the Austrian railway network. Scouts and Guides from neighbouring countries then collect their own light and take it home.

Over the years this has spread to other European countries and even as far as Russia. It first came to the UK in 1996 and created so much interest that it has continued each year since and has become a focal point in carol services, hospitals and homes.

The hope is that in passing on The Peace Light, its message of peace will spread to all countries and remain with us long after the lights have been extinguished.

WEDNESDAY — DECEMBER 17.

MY American friend, Wilma, keeps a box on her dresser into which she puts favourite quotations. She also keeps small trinkets there and a beautiful marble given to her by her son.

When she has problems or feels in need of inspiration, she reaches into the box and takes something out. Whatever it happens to be, it somehow puts her in touch with her own wisdom.

It seems a delightful idea and one we could all adopt. Now, what would you choose to put into your inspiration box?

THURSDAY — DECEMBER 18.

LIKE most people, the Lady of the House and I spend many days in a whirl of activity as we prepare for Christmas. We decorate the house and our tree, shop, bake, write cards and post presents. So I was surprised one year when she pointed out that so far there was one thing we had quite neglected to do.

"Can't you guess, Francis?" she laughed, seeing my puzzled face. "We have been forgetting to simply stop and take time to enjoy it all."

So we decided to postpone all our non-urgent chores and sat by the fireside instead, listening to carols on the radio and reflecting quietly on the real meaning of Christmas. I do hope that however busy you may be this year, you, too, can manage to glean a few moments just for yourself.

It's a gift far more precious than anything to be found in the shops!

SHEPHERD'S
DELIGHT

FRIDAY — DECEMBER 19.

I WAS once passing through a coach station when I saw a mother saying goodbye to her student daughter, obviously en route to a distant city. Both were tearful, behaving as if they were never going to see each other again, and I felt like reassuring them that their parting wasn't forever.

The writer Richard Bach put it well when he said: "Don't be dismayed at goodbyes. A farewell is necessary before you can meet again. And meeting again, after moments or lifetimes, is certain for those who are friends."

SATURDAY — DECEMBER 20.

ONE Christmas Eve just before the outbreak of the Second World War, an Australian radio announcer by the name of Norman Banks was sitting in the window of his Melbourne flat. From an open window across the street, he clearly heard a radio playing a Christmas carol. He glanced across — and noticed something else.

An old lady, with an expression of rapt attention on her face, was listening to the Christmas music. And, as she listened, she was holding a candle in her hand.

This fired the listener's imagination — and was the genesis of "Carols By Candlelight", now so familiar in many churches during the Christmas season. Christmas carols have been sung for hundreds of years, but only since 1937 have we enjoyed "Carols By Candlelight", a tradition surely worth cherishing.

THE FRIENDSHIP BOOK

SUNDAY — DECEMBER 21.

WHEN they had heard the king, they departed; and, lo, the star, which they saw in the east, went before them, till it came and stood over where the young child was.

Matthew 2:9

MONDAY — DECEMBER 22.

THESE words from "One Who Was", the autobiography of the late Brian Johnston, the well-loved cricket commentator and wit, who also wrote sympathetically on topics far removed from cricket, impressed me:

"I lay great store on kindness. My judgment of people is largely based on whether they are kind to their fellow human beings, especially to the old and to children, and not at the least to animals. My practical Christianity is based on the character in Charles Kingsley's 'Water Babies', Mrs Do-As-You-Would-Be-Done-By.

"It's a wonderful goal to aim at, and if everyone in the world would do as they would be done by, so many problems would be solved."

TUESDAY — DECEMBER 23.

CHILDREN are famous for getting right to the point. When little Laura's grandmother, trying to instil the real spirit of Christmas, asked why church bells ring on December 25th, quick as a flash came back the answer:

"Because the bellringer's pulling the rope!"

WEDNESDAY — DECEMBER 24.

LOOKING through some old magazines, I found an article about lunar rainbows. They are evidently very rarely seen. In the following issue, there were a few letters from people saying that they had been lucky enough to see one.

One gentleman wrote that his young son always told him that Santa Claus arrives by sliding his sleigh down the rainbow. One Christmas Eve they were walking to the service at church about seven o'clock in the evening. It was raining, but there in the western sky was a white rainbow created by the brilliant moon. He added that it was no surprise to his son, but a great delight to himself.

What an unusual way of remembering a Christmas Eve, and what a glorious way to start a New Year — at the beginning of a clean white rainbow. There must indeed be something good at the end of every rainbow. The little boy had faith that there is — and so should we.

THURSDAY — DECEMBER 25.

CAROLS by candlelight heartily sung,
 Holly and mistletoe lovingly hung,
The turkey is ready, mince pies are made,
 Pudding is steaming, table is laid.
Tree in the corner with twinkling lights,
 Heartwarming scene giving fancy her flights,
Such wonderful things here simply to say,
 Gentle Lord Jesus it's your special day.

Brian Hope Gent.

SEASON'S
GREETINGS

THE FRIENDSHIP BOOK

FRIDAY — DECEMBER 26.

PERCY VERANCE, Ernest N. Devvor, Will Power and Luke Lively. . . All are fictitious names, but there's certainly nothing imaginary about their potential as good companions on the journey through life.

SATURDAY — DECEMBER 27.

NEWLY-FALLEN SNOW

S ILENTLY the snowflakes fall
Like wisps of dainty lace,
Featherlike they flutter down
And brush against my face.
Gliding gently through the air
They're caught up in the breeze,
Then settle on the branches
Of frozen leafless trees.

Mother Nature comes to spread
Her beauty all around,
And leaves a blanket crisp and white
Of snowflakes on the ground.
There is a sense of silent awe
Of wonderment and peace,
As all the earth lies quiet and still
Beneath its icy fleece.

Kathleen Gillum.

SUNDAY — DECEMBER 28

FOR we walk by faith, not sight.

Corinthians II 5:7

MONDAY — DECEMBER 29.

*L*ORD, as the year draws to a close,
   Thank You for so many things:
For home and friendship, warmth and food
   And all each new day brings,
For all the guidance and the help,
   The things we have achieved,
For comfort, hope and kindness,
   The healing we've received.

Lord, thank You for the love we share,
   It grows with every day,
And like a beacon in the dark
   Will light our future way.
Now, as the year draws to a close,
   Lord, be our guard and guide,
And in the year which lies ahead
   Be always by our side.
                 Iris Hesselden.

TUESDAY — DECEMBER 30.

ONE ancient, yet ever-new, definition of friendship is that it is nothing more or less than "one soul in two bodies."

WEDNESDAY — DECEMBER 31.

HERE are two thoughts for New Year: never lose a chance to tell someone you love them!
And never accept a closed door in life; push it open, if you want to pass through and experience what lies on the other side.

The Photographers

Marcello Aita;
Reach For The Sky.
Terence J. Burchell;
Winter's Mantle.
Chris Cole;
Two's Company, The Way Ahead.
Paul Felix;
Tower of Strength, Horsepower.
Alex Gillespie;
Peaks Of Perfection, At Ease.
Regine Godfrey;
The Right Note, Buds and Blooms.
V. K. Guy;
Nature's Carpet, Well Earned Rest, House Proud.
Dennis Hardley;
The Hand Of Friendship, Past And Present.
T. G. Hopewell;
Garden Centre.
C. R. Kilvington;
Golden Glade.
Genevieve Leaper;
Shepherd's Delight.
Malcolm Nash;
Either Way Up.
Polly Pullar;
Perfect Perch.
Clifford Robinson;
Weed Like To Say Hello!
Willie Shand;
Wheely Delightful, Chapter And Verse.
Sheila Taylor;
Symphony In Spring, Season's Greetings.
Richard Watson;
Heaven Sent, Meadow Sweet.
Andy Williams;
Capital Crescendo, Mix And Match, Christmas Cheer.

Printed and Published by D. C. Thomson & Co., Ltd.,
185 Fleet Street, London EC4A 2HS.
ISBN 0-85116-820-5

THE Alphabet OF LIFE

Apply an optimistic trait.
Be conscious of the whims of Fate.
Capture comfort when you can.
Destroy each pessimistic plan.
Embark upon this theme, and choose
Friendship for a constant cruise.
Grab each opportunity that may
Help to brighten up the day.
It's never wise to analyse
Joys as some elusive prize.
Keep a level head although
Life can sometimes lay us low.
Misery deserves no vote —
Never let it rock the boat.
Organise a moral mix
Prepared to tackle trouble's tricks.
Question attitudes that bring
Rancour into everything.
Sincerity can help to make
Toleration's 'give and take'.
Understanding starts with 'U' —
Vindicate that point of view.
Wipe out lethargy a lot —
X can mark that special spot.
You can find, without regret,
Zest for living's alphabet.

J.M. Robertson